D1003601

How The Fierce Handle Fear

Secrets to Succeeding
in Challenging Times

How The Fierce Handle Fear

Secrets to Succeeding in Challenging Times

Edited by

Sophfronia Scott

Copyright 2010 by Sophfronia Scott. All rights reserved.

No part of this book may be reproduced or transmitted in any form or by any means, graphic, electronic, or mechanical, including photocopying, recording, taping, or by any information storage retrieval system, without the permission, in writing, from the publisher.

Two Harbors Press
212 3rd Ave N, Suite 290
Minneapolis, MN 55401
1-888-MILL CITY
www.millcitypress.net

ISBN 13: 978-1-936198-36-8
ISBN 10: 1-936198-36-3
LCCN: 2010928164

Printed in the United States of America
Book design by Wendy Arakawa

Cover Photo Credits - Canfield: Deborah Feingold, Trump: Vanguard Press, Slim: Ivan Martinez Photography, McKinney: Frank McKinney (private collection), Phillips: Jinsey Dauk, Arrato: Debra Arrato (private collection), Blackert: Jeneth Blackert (private collection), Ceniza-Levine: Caroline Ceniza-Levine (private collection), Carew: Cherry-Ann Carew (private collection), Glass: Sandie Glass (private collection), Johnson: Gretchel Johnson (private collection), Kay: Howard Kay (private collection), LeBlanc: Rachelle LeBlanc (private collection), Lee: Andrea J. Lee (private collection), Lindholm: Deborah Lindholm (private collection), McAuley: Jordan McAuley (private collection), Rao: Arathi R. Rao (private collection), Slack: Janet Slack (private collection), West: Darren West (private collection), Whelan: Joan Marie Whelan (private collection), Willis: Valarie Willis (private collection), Wishom: Laureen Wishom (private collection), Scott: Chia Messina

This book is dedicated to all who have ever been held back by a moment of fear. It is meant to be a key that will open the door to many cages so that those within can be free to reach their fullest potential.

Acknowledgments

Thank you to every single co-author in this book. I know I was asking for a lot, especially when it was clear that many of you had to dig down deep and revisit experiences and memories that were not pleasant. But the fact that you could do so only confirmed my conviction that we had the right people in this book. Your stories will undoubtedly touch many who will see themselves in what you wrote. Maybe they are now mired in the same hole, the same fearful situation that once held you. You get to be the friend who, as the Hosea Parable tells us, jumps down into the hole with them and says, "Don't worry. I've been down here before and I know the way out." Congratulations on your mastery of fear. Congratulations on stepping up to being the light to show the way.

Table of Contents

In Daily Life

With Spirituality

Introduction

I clearly remember the moment I learned what it felt like to let go of my fear. I was about 12 or 13, and my sister and I had gone to the store on our tandem bike for groceries. On the way home we took a corner too fast and the milk flew out of our basket and broke open on the street. We knew we were going to "get it". Our father wielded the belt frequently, and we often lived in fear of receiving a "whipping".

But that day as I watched the milk flowing down the street I remember a kind of fire burning within me. I was tired of being afraid. I was tired of gripping my insides so tightly as though I were already feeling the sting of the belt on my skin. I couldn't conjure that feeling anymore and I refused to try. I was done being fearful. It was like I had been carrying around a huge boulder and was finally putting it down.

"Come on," I said to my sister who, I could see, was very afraid. "Let's go home."

Honestly, I can't remember whether or not we did get the belt that day. I think it's because I really didn't care anymore--I probably endured whatever had happened and then gone on with the rest of the day. But that moment has stuck with me because as an adult I recognize it as a seminal one in my life. I see it reflected whenever situations come up when others are afraid, or afraid of someone, and I am not. Since I know what a burden fear can be, I tend to make a conscious choice not to take it on.

Until recently I've taken that choice, or rather, my ability to make that choice, for granted. One of my fellow entrepreneurs, gripped with worry about the economy, swine flu and a host of other issues of the world had asked me, "How can you not be afraid?" I told her, "It's just easier not to be. Being afraid is tiring! It takes a lot of work and energy." I made it clear I'd rather spend that energy elsewhere.

But her question stayed with me because I saw her fear being played back to me in the media and in the actions of many people reacting in fear to every single thing going on right now. I thought, "I can't see someone like Donald Trump reacting this way. He's too fierce. *This is not how fierce people handle fear.*"

Then it occurred to me: the average person doesn't know that. They just see people like a Donald Trump or a Debbie Phillips or a Jack Canfield behaving fearlessly, but they think the person is just that way—they don't see the work or the deep thinking that has brought them to where they are today. That's why I decided to assemble this book.

What makes these co-authors fierce? I believe a person is being fierce whenever he or she makes the effort to stand up for who they are and what they want in the face of everyday difficulties. With some of the co-authors, this fierceness is apparent in their very look—real estate maverick Frank McKinney wears his long blonde hair as fearlessly as he builds multi-million dollar homes. But for life coach Janet Slack, her fierceness is within and only revealed when you learn of how she rebuilt her life after a devastating tragedy.

I felt it was important for this book to have a mix of names you may recognize and names you don't so you'll be that much more likely to find a voice or a story you'll connect with. The co-authors of this book are of both sexes and of different ages, races and backgrounds. They have many different pieces of the puzzle to offer. I hope you'll find the piece that may be missing for you so you can put together your own model of fierceness.

Learning how to handle fear, I believe, is one of the most important skills we can master. The author Matthew Kelly, in his insightful program, *Living Every Day with Passion and Purpose*, points out that the phrase "Do not be afraid," appears over a thousand times in the Bible, words often attributed to God Himself. Why is that? Because, as Mr. Kelly says, "God knows the measure of our life is the measure of our courage."

I believe he's right, and that's why I felt this book is the most important book I could bring into the world right now. I hope it helps. The measure of your life will be the measure of your courage. It is up to you to decide whether you are up to the challenge or whether you will fall short. But I will tell you this: I believe you can measure up to be far greater than you imagine. This book is my gift to you so you may realize that.

Sophfronia Scott
Executive Editor
www.DoneForYouWriting.com

"Feel the Fear and Do It Anyway" from The Success Principles ™
by Jack Canfield and Janet Switzer
Copyright © 2005 by Jack Canfield
Reprinted by permission of HarperCollins Publishers

• • •

"Confronting Your Fears" from Think Like a Champion by
Donald J. Trump
Copyright © 2009 by Donald J. Trump
Reprinted by permission of Vanguard Press, a member of Perseus Books
Group

• • •

"Get off Your Knees and Start Walking" from The Tap by
Frank McKinney
Copyright © 2009 by Frank McKinney
Reprinted by permission of the author.

Proceeds from sales of this book go to benefit the good works of Frank McKinney's Caring House Project Foundation. CHPF endeavors to provide housing, food, water, medical support and opportunity for the desperately poor and homeless from around the world, particularly in the Caribbean, South America, Indonesia, Africa and the United States. To learn more about the program and how to make your own contribution please visit: http://www.frank-mckinney.com/caring_project.aspx

How the Fierce Handle Fear...

The Basics

Feel the Fear
and Do It Anyway
Jack Canfield

W*e come this way but once. We can either tiptoe through life and hope that we get to death without being too badly bruised or we can live a full, complete life achieving our goals and realizing our wildest dreams.*
Bob Proctor, Self-made millionaire, radio and TV personality, and success trainer

I have insecurities. But whatever I'm insecure about, I don't dissect it, but I'll go after it and say, "What am I afraid of?" I bet the average successful person can tell you they've failed so much more than they've had success. I've had far more failures than I've had successes. With every commercial I've gotten, there were 200 I didn't get. You have to go after what you're afraid of.
Kevin Sorbo, Actor who starred in the television series *Hercules: The Legendary Journeys*

As you move forward on your journey from where you are to where you want to be, you are going to have to confront your fears. Fear is natural. Whenever you start a new project, take on a new venture, or put yourself out there, there is usually fear. Unfortunately, most people let fear stop them from taking the necessary steps to achieve their dreams. Successful people, on the other hand, feel the fear along with the rest of us but don't let it keep them from doing anything they want to do—*or have to do.* They understand that fear is something to be acknowledged, experienced, and taken along for the ride. They have learned, as author Susan Jeffers suggests, to feel the fear and do it anyway.

Why Are We So Fearful?

Millions of years ago, fear was our body's way of signaling us that we were out of our comfort zone. It alerted us to possible danger, and gave us the burst of adrenaline we needed to run away. Unfortunately, though this response was useful in the days when saber-toothed tigers were chasing us, today most of our threats are not all that life-threatening.

Today, fear is more of a signal that we must stay alert and cautious. We can feel fear, but we can still move forward anyway. Think of your fear as a 2-year-old child who doesn't want to go grocery shopping with you. You wouldn't let a 2-year-old's mentality run your life. Because you must buy groceries, you'll just have to take the 2-year-old along with you. Fear is no different. In other words, acknowledge that fear exists but don't let it keep you from doing important tasks.

You Have to Be Willing to Feel the Fear

Some people will do anything to avoid the uncomfortable feeling of fear. If you are one of those people, you run an even bigger risk of never getting what you want in life. Most of the good stuff requires taking a risk. And the nature of a risk is that it doesn't always work out. People do lose their investments, people do forget their lines, people do fall off mountains, people do die in accidents. But as the old adage so wisely tells us, "Nothing ventured, nothing gained."

When I interviewed Jeff Arch, who wrote the screenplay for the movie

Sleepless in Seattle, he told me:

I am about to launch the biggest gamble of my life—writing and directing a two-million-dollar comedy, when I have never directed before, and using my own money plus raising other money to fund it—and I really need to succeed at this. Really, it's an all-or-nothing situation. And the thing that I'm experiencing right now, which I think is really important and that a lot of people who write about success leave out, is you've got to be willing to be terrified. Because I am terrified about what I'm about to do. But it's not immobilizing. It's a good terrified; it's a terrified that keeps you on your toes.

I know I have to do this because I had a very clear vision, and I am willing to stand alone without agreement from the industry, which I learned you have to do from when I was pitching *Sleepless in Seattle*. Believe me, when you start pitching an idea about a love story where the lead characters don't meet, you are alone. Everybody told me, "You're out of your freaking mind." And one thing I discovered is when everyone says you're out of your mind, you just might be on to something. So, I had these reference points from my past experience. I was alone back then. And I was right. I've learned you have to believe in your dream. Because even if everyone is telling you you're wrong, that still might not mean anything—you just might be right.

You reach a point where you say, "This is it. I'm throwing everything into this. And it's got to succeed." It's like the Spanish conquistador Hernando Cortez in 1519. To prevent any thought of retreating from his mission, after he landed in Mexico, he burned all of his ships. Well, I've rented new ships just for the sake of burning them. I took out loans on ships that weren't even mine. I'm throwing money, credibility—every single thing there is—into my new project. And it's either going to be a home run or a strikeout—not a single or a double.

I know there's a terror in doing this, but there's also this confidence. It isn't going to kill me. It might make me broke, it might leave me in debt, it might make me lose credibility, and it might make the journey back a whole lot harder. But unlike Cortez, I'm not in a business where they kill you if you goof up. I think one of the secrets to my success is that I'm willing to be terrified, and I think a lot of people are not willing to be scared to death. And that's why they don't achieve the big dream.

Fantasized Experiences Appearing Real

Another important aspect to remember about fear is that, as humans, we've also evolved to the stage where almost all of our fears are now self-created. We frighten ourselves by fantasizing negative outcomes to any activity we might pursue or experience. Luckily, because we are the ones doing the fantasizing, we are also the ones who can stop the fear and bring ourselves into a state of clarity and peace by facing the actual facts, rather than giving in to our imaginations. We can choose to be sensible. Psychologists like to say that *fear* means

Fantasized

Experiences

Appearing

Real

To help you better understand how we actually bring unfounded fear into our lives, make a list of things you are afraid to *do*. This is not a list of things you are afraid *of*, such as being afraid *of* spiders, but things you're afraid to *do*, such as being afraid to pick up a spider. For example, *I am afraid to*

Ask my boss for a raise

Ask Sally out for a date

Go skydiving

Leave my kids home alone with a sitter

Leave this job that I hate

Take 2 weeks away from the office

Ask my friends to look at my new business opportunity

Delegate any part of my job to others

Now go back and restate each fear using the following format:

I want to _____, and I scare myself by imagining_____.

The key words are *I scare myself by imagining.* All fear is self-created by imagining some negative outcome in the future. Using some of the same fears listed above, the new format would look like this:

I want to ask my boss for a raise, and I scare myself by imagining he would say no and be angry with me for asking.

I want to ask Sally out for a date, and I scare myself by imagining that she would say no and I would feel embarrassed.

I want to go skydiving, and I scare myself by imagining that my parachute wouldn't open and I would be killed.

I want to leave my kids home with a sitter, and I scare myself by imagining that something terrible would happen to them.

I want to leave this job I hate to pursue my dream, and I scare myself by imagining I would go bankrupt and lose my house.

I want to ask my friends to look at my new business opportunity, and I scare myself by imagining they will think I am only interested in making money off of them.

Can you see that you are the one creating the fear?

How to Get Rid of Fear

I have lived a long life and had many troubles, most of which never happened.

Mark Twain, Celebrated American author and humorist

One way to actually *disappear* your fear is to ask yourself what you're imagining that is scary to you, and then replace that image with its positive opposite.

When I was flying to Orlando recently to give a talk, I noticed the woman next to me was gripping the arms of her seat so tightly her knuckles were turning white. I introduced myself, told her I was a trainer, and said I couldn't help but notice her hands. I asked her, "Are you afraid?"

"Yes."

"Would you be willing to close your eyes and tell me what thoughts or images you are experiencing in your head?"

After she closed her eyes, she replied, "I just keep imagining the plane not getting off the runway and crashing."

"I see. Tell me, what are you headed to Orlando for?"

"I'm going there to spend four days with my grandchildren at Disney World."

"Great. What's your favorite ride at Disney World?"

"It's a Small World."

"Wonderful. Can you imagine being at Disney World in one of the gondolas with your grandchildren in the It's a Small World attraction?"

"Yes."

"Can you see the smiles and the looks of wonder on your grandchildren's faces as they watch all the little puppets and figures from the different countries bobbing up and down and spinning around?"

"Uh-huh."

At that point I started to sing, "It's a small world after all; it's a small world after all…"

Her face relaxed, her breathing deepened, and her hands released their grip on the arms of the seat.

In her mind, she was already at Disney World. She had replaced the catastrophic picture of the plane crashing with a positive image of her desired outcome, and instantly her fear disappeared.

You can use this same technique to disappear any fear that you might ever experience.

Replace the Physical Sensations Fear Brings

Did you ever learn to dive off a diving board? If so, you probably remember the first time you walked to the edge of the board and looked down. The water looked a lot deeper than it really was. And considering the height of the board and the height of your eyes above the board, it probably looked like a *very* long way down.

You were scared. But did you look at your mom or dad or the diving instructor and say, "You know, I'm just too afraid to do this right now. I think I'll go do some therapy on this, and if I can get rid of my fear, I'll come back and try again…"?

No! You didn't say that.

You felt the fear, somehow mustered up courage from somewhere, and jumped into the water. You felt the fear and did it anyway.

When you surfaced, you probably swam like crazy to the side of the pool and took a few well-earned deep breaths. Somewhere, there was a little rush of adrenaline, the thrill of having survived a risk, plus the thrill of jumping through the air into the water. After a minute, you probably did it again, and then again and again—enough to where it got to be really fun. Pretty soon, all of the fear was gone and you were doing cannonballs to splash your friends and maybe even learning how to do a back flip.

If you can remember that experience or the first time you drove a car or the first time you kissed someone on a date, you've got the model for everything that happens in life. New experiences will always feel a little scary. They're supposed to. That's the way it works. But every time you face a fear and do it anyway, you build up that much more confidence in your abilities.

Scale Down the Risk

Anthony Robbins says, "If you can't, you must, and if you must, you can." I agree. It is those very things that we are most afraid to do that provide the greatest liberation and growth for us.

If a fear is so big that it paralyzes you, scale down the amount of risk. Take on smaller challenges and work your way up. If you're starting your first job in sales, call on prospects or customers you think will be the easiest to sell to first. If you're asking for money for your business, practice on those lending sources that you wouldn't want to get a loan from anyway. If you're anxious about taking on new responsibilities at work, start by asking to do parts of a project you're interested in. If you're learning a new sport, start at lower levels of skill. Master those skills you need to learn, move through your fears and then take on bigger challenges.

When Your Fear is Really a Phobia

Some fears are so strong that they can actually immobilize you. If you have a full-blown phobia, such as fear of flying or fear of being in an elevator, it can seriously inhibit your ability to be successful. Fortunately there is a simple solution for most phobias. The Five-Minute Phobia Cure, developed by Dr. Roger Callahan, is easy to learn and can be self-administered as well as facilitated by a professional.

I learned about this magical technique from Dr. Callahan's book and video and have used it successfully in my seminars for more than 15 years. The process uses a simple but precise pattern of tapping on various points of the body while you simultaneously imagine the object or experience that stimulates your phobic reaction. It acts in much the same way as a virus in a computer program by permanently interrupting the "program" or sequence of events that occur in the brain between the initial sighting of the thing you are afraid of (such as seeing a snake or stepping into an airplane) and the physical response (such as sweating, shaking, shallow breathing, or weak knees) you experience.

When I was leading a seminar for real estate agents, a woman revealed that she had a phobia about walking up stairs. In fact, she had experienced it that very morning, when in response to her request for directions to the seminar, the bellman had pointed to a huge staircase leading to the grand ballroom. Fortunately, there was also an elevator, so she made it to the seminar. If there hadn't been, she would have turned around and driven home. She admitted that she had never been on the second floor of any home she had ever sold. She would pretend she had already been up there, tell the prospective buyers what they would find on the second floor, on the basis of her reading the listing sheet, and then let them explore it on their own.

I did the Five-Minute Phobia Cure with her and then took all 100 people out to the same hotel stairway that had petrified her earlier in the day. With no hesitation, heavy breathing, or drama, she walked up and down the stairs twice. It is that simple.

Take a Leap!

Come to the edge, He said.
They said: We are afraid.
Come to the edge, He said.
They came. He pushed them,
And they flew…
Guillaume Apollinaire, Avant-garde French poet

All the successful people I know have been willing to take a chance—a leap of faith—even though they were afraid. Sometimes they were terrified, but they knew if they didn't act, the opportunity would pass them by. They trusted their intuition and they simply went for it.

Progress always involves risk; you can't steal second base and keep your foot on first.
Frederick Wilcox

Mike Kelley lives in paradise and owns several companies under the umbrella of Beach Activities of Maui. With only a year of college under his belt (he never did return to get his degree), Mike left Las Vegas at age 19 for the islands of Hawaii and ended up selling suntan lotion by the pool at a hotel in Maui. From these humble beginnings, Mike went on to create a company with 175 employees and over $5 million in annual revenues that provides recreational experiences (catamaran and scuba diving excursions) for tourists and concierge services and business centers for many of the island's hotels.

Mike credits much of his success to always being willing to take a leap when needed. When Beach Activities of Maui was attempting to expand its business, there was an important hotel whose business he wanted, but a competitor had held the contract for over 15 years. To maintain a competitive edge, Mike always reads the trade journals and keeps an ear open to what is happening in his business. One day he read that this hotel was changing general managers, and the new general manager who would be coming in lived in Copper Mountain, Colorado. This got Mike to thinking: Because it is so hard to get through all of the gatekeepers to secure a meeting with a general manager, maybe he should try to contact him before he actually moved to Hawaii. Mike wrestled with what would be the best way to contact him. Should he write a letter? Should he call him on the phone? As he pondered these options, his friend Doug suggested, "Why don't you just hop on a plane and go see him?"

Always one to take action and take it now, Mike quickly put together a pro forma and a proposal and hopped on a plane the next night. After flying all night, he arrived in Colorado, rented a car and drove the 2 hours out to Copper Mountain, and showed up unannounced at the new general manager's office. He explained who he was, congratulated him on his new promotion, told him that he looked forward to having him in Maui, and asked for a few moments to tell him about his company and what it could do for his hotel.

Mike didn't get the contract during that first meeting, but the fact that a young kid was so confident in himself and his services that he would take a leap of faith to jump on a plane and fly all the way to Denver and drive out into the middle of Colorado on the off chance that he would be able to get together with him left such a huge impression on the general manager that when he did finally get to Hawaii, Mike secured the contract, which, over the ensuing 15 years, has been worth hundreds of thousands of dollars to Mike's bottom line.

Taking a Leap Can Transform Your Life

Authority is 20% given and 80% taken…so take it!
Peter Ueberroth, Organizer of the 1984 Summer Olympics and
commissioner of Major League Baseball, 1984-1988

Multimillionaire Dr. John Demartini is a resounding success by anyone's standards. He's married to a beautiful and brilliant woman—Athena Starwoman, the world-famous astrologer who consults and writes for 24 well-known magazines, including *Vogue*. Together, they own several homes in Australia. And they spend over 60 days a year together circumnavigating the globe in their $3 million luxury apartment onboard the $550 million ocean liner *World of ResidenSea*—a residence they purchased after selling their Trump Tower apartment in New York City.

The author of 54 training programs and 13 books, John spends the year traveling the world speaking and conducting his courses on financial success and life mastery.

But John didn't start out rich and successful. At age 7, he was found to have a learning disability and was told that he would never read, write, or communicate normally. At 14, he dropped out of school, left his Texas home, and headed for the California coast. By 17, he had ended up in Hawaii, surfing the waves of Oahu's famed North Shore, where he almost died from strychnine poisoning. His road to recovery led him to Dr. Paul Bragg, a 93-year-old man who changed John's life by giving him one simple affirmation to repeat: "I am a genius and I apply my wisdom."

Inspired by Dr. Bragg, John went to college, earned his bachelor's degree from the University of Houston and later his doctoral degree from the Texas College of Chiropractic.

When he opened his first chiropractic office in Houston, John started with just 970 square feet of space. Within 9 months, he'd more than doubled that and was offering free classes on healthy living. When attendance grew, John was ready to expand again. It was then he took a leap that changed his career forever.

"It was Monday," John said. "The shoe store next door had vacated over the weekend." *What a perfect lecture hall,* John thought as he quickly phoned the leasing company.

When no one called him back, John concluded they weren't going to rent the space soon, so he took a leap.

"I called a locksmith to come out and open up the place," John said. "I thought the worst thing they would do was charge me the rent."

He quickly transformed the space into a lecture hall and within days was holding free talks there on a nightly basis. Because the space was located right next to a movie theater, he added a loudspeaker so moviegoers could hear his lectures as they walked to their cars. Hundreds began attending classes and eventually became patients.

John's practice grew rapidly. Yet nearly 6 months went by before the property manager came to investigate.

"You've got a lot of courage," the manager said. "You remind me of me." In fact, he was so impressed with John's daring, he even gave John 6 months' free rent! "Anybody that has the courage to do what you did deserves it," he told him. The manager later invited John down to his office, where he offered him a quarter of a million dollars a year to come work for him. John turned it down because he had other plans, but it was a huge validation of his courage to act.

Taking a leap helped John build a thriving practice, which he later sold to begin consulting full time with other chiropractors.

"Taking that leap opened up a doorway for me," John said. "If I'd held back...if I had been cautious...I wouldn't have made the breakthrough that gave me the life I live today."

Oh, What the Heck—Just Go For It!

Do you want to be safe and good, or do you want to take a chance and be great?

Jimmy Johnson, Coach who led the Dallas Cowboys football team to two consecutive Super Bowl championships in 1992 and 1993

When Richard Paul Evans wrote his first book, *The Christmas Box*, it was simply a gift of love to his two young daughters. Later, he made photocopies for family and friends, and word spread quickly about this heartwarming tale. Spurred on by this positive reaction, Rick sought a publisher for the book. When there were no takers, Rick decided to publish it himself.

To promote the book, he took a booth at a regional American Booksellers Association conference, where, among other activities, celebrity authors were signing books at one end of the exhibit hall. Rick noticed these celebrity authors were the only ones getting attention from the press. He also noticed that when the next group of celebrities arrived for their scheduled time, one author had failed to arrive.

With his fear being crowded out by his courage and commitment to his dream, Rich decided to take a leap. He picked up two boxes of books, walked toward the empty chair, sat down, and began to sign.

Seeing him at the table, a woman from the show approached him to ask him to leave. Undaunted, Evans looked up and before she could speak said, "Sorry I'm late." The stunned woman just looked at him and asked, "Can I get you something to drink?" The next year, Evans was the premier author at the show as his book climbed to number 1 on the *New York Times* Best-Seller List. Since then, *The Christmas Box* has sold more than 8 million copies in 18 languages and has been made into an Emmy Award-winning CBS television movie. The book, which had been previously rejected by several major publishing houses, was eventually purchased by Simon & Schuster for a record $4.2 million.

Living at risk is jumping off the cliff and building your wings on the way down.
Ray Bradbury, Author of more than 500 literary works

Be Willing to Put It All on the Line for Your Dream

Only those who dare to fail greatly can ever achieve greatly.
Robert F. Kennedy, Former attorney general and U.S. senator

In January of 1981, real estate investor Robert Allen took a challenge—putting it all on the line—that would make or break his new career as an author and seminar leader. He was looking for ways to promote his book *Nothing Down: How to Buy Real Estate with Little or No Money Down.* Frustrated with the ad his publisher's public relations department had created, Bob found himself spouting off the top of his head what he felt needed to be said in the ad. "We need to demonstrate that someone can buy property with nothing down."

His publisher responded, "What do you mean?"
Bob said, "I don't know. You could take me to a city, take away my wallet and give me a hundred bucks, and I'd buy a property."

"How long would it take you?"

"I don't know, maybe a week, maybe three or four days—seventy-two hours."

"Can you do that?"

Bob found himself looking at the abyss, realizing he'd never done that before and not knowing for sure if he could do it now. He head was saying no and his heart was saying yes.

Bob went with his heart and said, "Yeah, I probably can do that."

"Well, if you can do that, that's the title of the ad we're going to run: 'So then he said he'd take away my wallet, give me a hundred-dollar bill, and send me out to buy a piece of real estate using none of my own money.'"

Bob said, "Okay, let it rip," and they ran the ad, which was very successful. Within a few months after being released, the book was number one on the *Time* magazine bestseller list and it ended up being on the *New York Times* Best-Seller List for 46 weeks.

Later that year Bob got a call from a reporter at the *Los Angeles Times* who said, "We don't think you can do what you say you can do."

Bob replied, "Well, I'd be glad to be challenged," and then quipped, "How about a date sometime in 2050?" But the *Times* was serious—serious about taking Bob down. The reporter said, "I am going to take you down. We don't like your ad. We think you're a fraud, and you're going down." Scared, but determined he had to take the challenge, Bob set it up for 4 weeks later.

On January 12, 1981, the reporter from the *Times* met him at the Marriott Hotel just east of Los Angeles International Airport. Bob hadn't slept much the night before. In fact, he hadn't slept much for the entire month before. He lay awake at night wondering if he could really pull it off in such a short time. Taking the challenge had felt like the right thing to do, but he still didn't know if he could do it.

Together they boarded a plane and flew to San Francisco, and Bob hit the ground running. He immediately went to a real estate office and started writing no-money-down-offers, and they promptly escorted them out of the office, which Bob recalls, "was not a good way to start."

Bob started thinking, "*Uh-oh, I'm in deep trouble now. I'm going to lose it all. It's gone. I'm not going to be able to pull this off. What was I thinking?*" Was he scared? "Oh yeah, I was terrified." But he just made call after call after call and finally, toward the end of the first day, he started running into some success and found a property that somebody was willing to sell him. By the next morning he had a signed offer.

So it had been just a little over 24 hours and he had bought his first property. Then Bob said, "We're not done yet. You gave me 72 hours. I've scheduled my life for this for the next 3 days. Let's see how many we can do." At this point, the reporter became his cheerleader. After all, the reporter had already lost the challenge, and the bigger he lost, the better the story.

Before, he was saying, "I'm going to take you down." Now it was, "Hey, Bob, go for it, boy. If you're going to beat me, beat me bad." And Bob did. He bought seven properties worth $700,000 in 57 hours and gave the reporter $20 back out of the $100 he had started with.

The subsequent article, which was syndicated by the *Los Angeles Times* and picked up by dozens of newspapers across the country, launched Bob's career. He had risked it all, and he had won big time! His book *Nothing Down* went on to sell over a million copies and became the eleventh best-selling hardcover book of the 1980s.

The Challenge

If you want to achieve a high goal, you're going to have to take some chances.
Alberto Salazar, Winner of three consecutive New York City Marathons

in 1980, 1981, and 1982, and now a spokesperson for Nike

Robert Allen's life seems to have been built on leaping into the void to prove that his methods can and do work—for everyone, no matter their status—to produce wealth and abundance in their lives. Even after his stunning success of buying seven houses in 72 hours with no money down in San Francisco, the press still hounded him with, "Well, sure, *you* can do it, but the average person couldn't do it." Bob's message was that *anybody* could buy property with no money down, but the press kept countering with "Well, you're not just anybody."

Bob told me, "I became so infuriated with the press that I said, 'You can send me to any unemployment line'—and I remember stuff just coming out of my mouth, not knowing where it was coming from—'let me select someone who's broke, out of work, and discouraged, and in two days time I'll teach him the secrets of wealth. And in ninety days he'll be back on his feet with five thousand dollars cash in the bank, and he'll never set foot in an unemployment line again.'"

Bob went to St. Louis, asked the ex-mayor to oversee the project, went to the unemployment office, and handed out 1,200 flyers offering to teach people how to become financially independent. Expecting the room to be filled to the rafters, he had the room set up for 300 chairs, but only 50 people showed up—and half those people left at the first break as soon as they heard how much work was going to be involved. After an extensive interview process, only three couples remained. He worked with those three couples. Though all of them did deals in the first 90 days, technically only one of them made the $5,000 cash in the 3-month period. All of them did more deals that year and changed their lives in a variety of different ways. The couple that made the $5,000 cash in the first 90 days went on to make over $100,000 in the next 12 months. Once again, taking a huge risk, by leaping into the void, Bob had proved his point and finally made the press back off.

He went on to write a book about the experience called *The Challenge*. While it was his least successful book, selling only 65,000 copies, it became his most profitable because it was the first book he ever put his name, address, and phone numbers in. Over 4,000 of the people who read that book called Bob's office and eventually paid $5,000 to attend Bob's ongoing training program. That's $20 million—not bad for being willing to pay the price of putting his butt on the line one more time.

The secret to my success is that I bit off more than I could chew and chewed as fast as I could.
Paul Hogan, Actor who portrayed Crocodile Dundee

High Intention...Low Attachment

If you want to remain calm and peaceful as you go through life, you have to have high intention and low attachment. You do everything you can to create your desired outcomes, and then you let it go. Sometimes you don't get the intended result by the date that you want. That is life. You just keep moving in the direction of your goal until you get there. Sometimes the universe has other plans, and often they are better than the ones you had in mind. That is why I recommend adding the phrase "this or something better" to the end of your affirmations.

When I was vacationing with my family on a cruise in Tahiti two summers ago, my son Christopher and my stepson Travis, both 12 at the time, and I set out on a guided bicycle tour around the island of Bora-Bora with some other members from our cruise ship. My intention for the day was a bonding experience with my two sons. The wind was blowing really hard that day and the trip was a difficult one. At one point, Stevie Eller, who was struggling along with her 11-year-old grandson, took a nasty fall and badly cut her leg. Because there were only a few others in the back of the pack with us, we stayed behind to help her. There were no homes or stores and virtually no traffic on the far side of the island, meaning that there was no way to call for help, so after attempting some crude first aid, we decided to all push on together. Bored with the slow pace, my boys took off ahead, and I spent the next several hours pedaling and walking next to my new friend until we eventually reached a hotel where she called for a taxi and I rejoined my sons, who had stopped for a swim, for the rest of the trip around the island. That night Stevie and her husband, Karl, asked us to join their family for dinner.

It turned out that they were on the nominating committee for the 2004 International Achievement Summit sponsored by the Academy of Achievement, whose mission was to "inspire youth with new dreams of achievement in a world of boundless opportunity" by bringing together over 200 university and graduate student delegates from around the world to interact with contemporary leaders who have achieved the difficult or impossible in service to their fellow humans. After our time together, they decided to nominate me to become a member of the academy and receive their Golden Plate Award, joining previous recipients such as former president Bill Clinton, Placido Domingo, George Lucas, New York mayor Rudolph Giuliani, U.S. senator John McCain, former prime minister of Israel Shimon Peres, and Archbishop Desmond Tutu. Because my nomination was accepted, I was able to attend the annual 4-day event with some of the brightest young future leaders and some of the most interesting and accomplished people in the world in 2004 and will be able to attend every year for the rest of my life—and I can even bring my sons to a future meeting!

Had I been totally attached to my original outcome of a day with my two sons and left Stevie to the care of others, I would have missed an even bigger opportunity that spontaneously came my way. I have learned over the years that whenever one door seemingly closes, another door opens. You just have to keep positive, stay aware, and look to see what it is. Instead of getting upset when things don't unfold as you anticipated, always ask yourself the question "What's the possibility that this is?"

*   *   *   *   *   *   *

Jack Canfield fostered the emergence of inspirational anthologies as a genre with his origination of the beloved ***Chicken Soup for the Soul*** franchise that has sold over 100 million books. Affectionately known as "America's #1 Success Coach", Jack has studied and reported on what makes successful people different. He knows what motivates them, what drives them, and what inspires them. He brings this critical insight to countless audiences internationally, sharing his success strategies with the media, with companies, universities and professional associations in over 20 countries around the world. His other books, ***The Success Principles, The Power of Focus, The Aladdin Factor*** and ***Dare to Win*** have generated millions of bookstore and internet sales and have launched complementary products such as audio programs, video programs, syndicated columns, coaching programs and branded retail merchandise. Jack holds the Guinness Book World Record for having seven books simultaneously on the *New York Times* Bestseller List--beating out Stephen King.

The Gift of Fear
Pamela Slim

My stomach clenched as I grabbed some more clothes and shoved them into a plastic shopping bag. I felt shaky, unstable, about to throw up. I steadied myself against the wall as I surveyed all the other things that needed to be packed.

It was impossible.

Leaving this awful relationship, giving up all that I had worked for was too much to bear.

I was terrified.

In this moment over a decade ago, I had never felt so much fear. It was all-encompassing, like living in an Alfred Hitchcock movie. My heart pounded in my ears, and time seemed to slow to a crawl.

But I pressed forward, eventually packing all of my things into my Mom's waiting VW van. As we pulled away from the curb, I felt a surge of relief. My shoulders relaxed and I felt my nausea subside.

Raising a glass of tea at my friend's house an hour later, I was on top of the world. All the fear was gone, and all I felt was tremendous, quiet power.

I had sparred with fear, feeling like a sickly child waving a cardboard sword against a fierce warrior with a gleaming sheath. And I won.

Courage follows, not leads fear

This experience showed me that the way popular culture views courage is all wrong. It is not an emotional state we need to attain before tackling something scary. Courage is the *result* of walking through fear and surviving it.

We try to steel our nerves and manifest courage, playing the theme song from *Rocky* in our head as we stare at the blank page on the computer screen that we wish to fill with 1500 words or eyeing the phone we need to use to make a cold call.

Trying to ignore the fear and push through it just serves to make it stronger. It turns from a small iguana into a flame-spitting three-headed dragon.

Instead, the best way to get through fear is to become acquainted with it.

Fear is not the enemy

The design of fear in our physiology is to keep us safe, warm and well-fed.

Baked deep in our brain is a message system that constantly alerts us to danger and prepares us to fight off or flee dangerous situations.

Rather than view it as a snarling beast to be slaughtered, I choose to see it like a sweet-smelling grandma who bakes apple pies and tucks a hand-stitched comforter under your chin while kissing you goodnight on your forehead.

She says, "I don't want anything bad to ever happen to you. I want you to make smart decisions and marry a man who will take care of you."

And like this sweet-spirited grandma, her sense of what is dangerous is not always in line with yours.

"You know what they say about that *Internet* dear, it is filled with scam artists and stalkers."

Or a favorite piece of grandma-like advice:

"The best thing to do when graduating from college is to pick a stable career path in a big company and work there until retirement."

We all know how well that advice is working today!

When you view fear as a protective force, and not a threat, your breathing slows and you are able to think more clearly.

How do you handle fear?

Since trying to appear courageous while quaking in our boots does nothing but increase the terror, here are five steps to successfully engage with fear:

Step 1: Recognize

The other day my four-year-old son was riding his bike on the sidewalk in our neighborhood. My two-year-old daughter was taking her time crossing the street with me, and I told my son to stop at the corner. Looking back to hold my daughter's hand, I took my eye off of him for a second. Suddenly, I looked up and saw a car backing out of the driveway right where he was peddling.

My stomach lurched to my throat and I screamed loudly.

He looked back at the car that had just missed hitting him.

"Sorry Mom!" he said, and kept peddling towards our house.

I shook for two hours.

My mind began to spin out of control.

I don't even like to articulate what I thought about. I brought myself to the darkest, scariest place a Mom could imagine.

Then I realized that I was in the grips of primal fear. Left in this state, my thoughts would run crazy, and I would never let my son outside the house again.

This physiological state: beating heart, dry mouth and tunnel vision is the sign that your inner protector is feeling extremely threatened.

Step 2: Listen

Once you realize you are engulfed in fear, you need to decipher the real from imagined dangers.

You may be surprised that fear talks to you, if you just let it. Approach it like sipping a hot cup of coffee with a dear friend:

"So, dear fear, what is this I hear about your desire to cut your heart out with a knife rather than face the truth that your marriage is troubled?"

It is most helpful to have this conversation with your fear in a place that feels safe and open.

Hours before packing my belongings in plastic bags and fleeing my bad relationship, I visited Phoenix Lake, a favorite haunt from my childhood. I went there right after work and walked around the whole lake in my cashmere sweater, velvet pants and pearls. And when I got to the place where I had gone as a young girl of seven years old to mourn my parent's divorce, I broke down sobbing.

In the midst of musky redwood trees and a babbling brook, I had found a safe place where I could admit the truth: I was in over my head. My relationship was so badly damaged that it was terrifying. I felt trapped, tortured and scared.

Depending on your particular situation, when you ask your fear what it is afraid of, it will say things like: "If you take your hand out of the bag of Oreos, you will never have access to food again, and you will starve to death on the kitchen floor."

"If you ask for a raise, you will get fired and be unable to take care of your family."

"If you stand up in the front of this room and give your presentation, everyone will realize you are a huge fraud and have nothing of value to say."

Your fears may need to be heard by a compassionate witness like a friend, spiritual advisor, coach or therapist, or you may choose to just say them to yourself.

But get them all out. Don't worry, they won't hurt you. In fact just by articulating them, you should start to feel much, much better.

Step 3: Decipher

Once the fears are out on the table, it is much easier to look at them with an objective eye.

Examine each one and ask yourself:

Is it true?

What is the worst that can happen if this comes to pass?

Would that be worse than staying in this situation?

What will happen if I don't confront this fear?

What or who would make me feel stronger, more supported or confident?

Do I know anyone who has faced a similar fear and come out safer and stronger?

What information do I need to challenge my perspective and see this from a different angle?

Has anyone ever died from doing this?

The more you examine your fears from different angles; the smaller and more specific they get.

Then you can start to test them in the real world.

Step 4: Test

Fear thrives when it is untested. So break down a specific fear into a tiny action and see if you survive completing it.

"You will fail miserably in business" can be broken into small tests like:

Will you fail miserably if you send one email to five of your close friends asking them if they know of anyone who can use your graphic design skills?

Will you fail miserably if you set up a PayPal account to accept payments for your graphic design business?

Will you fail miserably if you go to Wordpress.com and set up a one-page website with one paragraph about you and one paragraph about the services you offer?

Try it!

If you are like most people, you will find that not only do you survive these tiny tests, you actually gain courage and momentum by completing them.

Each time a piece of a large fear like "you will fail miserably in business" is proved wrong, it becomes less threatening. Your inner protector relaxes, and you have the energy to walk through the fear one step at a time.

Before you know it, you are on the other side of a tremendously frightening experience and can say with a bit of swagger, "Well, that wasn't so hard! What's next?"

Step 5: Thank

When you are safe and happy, basking in the thrill of taking on a challenge and surviving it, don't forget to thank your inner protector.

The more you strengthen the connection with your voice of fear, the more it will serve you in the future.

So in a quiet moment, however you want to express it, make sure you say something like:

"Thank you sweet grandma for looking out for my health and well-being! I know you want the best for me. Now how about a slice of warm apple pie?"

The gift

The blessing of writing this chapter, remembering that day of terror from today's vantage point of a happy and secure marriage, is that I realize intense fear always passes. Living through fear builds a solid base of trust and self-confidence.

I still feel fear in many parts of my life: as a parent, a child and a business owner. I swallow hard when I take on a new challenge, and question my sanity for stepping out of my comfort zone.

But I know that by stepping into fear, feeling it, talking with it and walking slowly through it does lead to the elation of post-terror courage.

And it is worth every shaky step.

*　　*　　*　　*　　*　　*　　*

Pamela Slim is a business coach and author of *Escape from Cubicle Nation: From Corporate Prisoner to Thriving Entrepreneur.* You can download the first chapter of her book at www.escapefromcubiclenation.com.

Fear, Fear On the Wall Who Is Fearless After All?
Debbie Phillips

The fear fluttered up from my stomach and filled my brain so quickly I thought I was going to faint.

I don't remember ever feeling this scared in my life. I was 9 years old and rehearsing on a stage for the first time. Dazzled after recently seeing performers at Holiday on Ice, I dreamed to be in a show…any show. And, here I was rehearsing steps for my first show, a folk-dance recital; my dreams come true. I was prepared. I had mastered the steps and knew them without fail.

How could I feel so absolutely terrified?

Out of the blue, my equally young dance partner whispered to me. "I heard that if you feel really nervous, there's an exercise that actresses use to get calm," she said with the confidence of an adult.

"You have to do it in private," she said. And, we slipped behind the red velvet curtain and she demonstrated.

"You make fists with your hands and then press them together, lining them up so your knuckles fit into each other. Then you press your fists together really hard and breathe into them for a few minutes. When you let go, you're no longer afraid."

I tried it. Wow. It worked! I felt calm and steady. My anxiety was under control. In fact, all would have gone smoothly and effortlessly had I not gotten the flu the day of the show and missed the entire performance!

What stayed with me from that experience so long ago is something way more valuable than simply coping with stage fright. I learned to believe that whenever I felt fear there must be a strategy, a technique, a method to relieve it.

*   *   *   *   *   *   *

Now that doesn't mean the fear-vanquishing solution I learned for 4th grade folk dancing would be a one-size-fits-all remedy for all future fears. Wish it were so.

No, life's many twists and turns required me to discover new ways to deal with fear. The fear and anxiety that comes from:
   * Losing a loved one
   * Managing an overwhelming job and career
   * Dealing with major disappointments and setbacks
   * Getting divorced
   * Finding life purpose
   * Facing a health or financial crisis
   * Encountering abuse, threats, violence, natural disasters
   * Experiencing world events out of control

*   *   *   *   *   *   *

Growing up in a small Ohio town and the oldest of five siblings, I believed I needed to be brave. I worried that if I cried or showed I was scared, it might frighten everyone else down the line. So, while I surely had my share of meltdowns and terrified moments as a kid, it was mostly after

I left home that I focused on handling the fear I often held inside.

I was in my 20s when I became aware of a major fear: I was not smart enough or capable enough. I was a newspaper reporter and later a staff member on a presidential candidate's campaign.

My fear of inadequacy drove me to work harder and longer to make up for what I perceived to be my lack of knowledge, experience or ability. It wore me ragged.

Yet, it led me to discover that physical exercise and time in nature or with animals could relieve my nervous mind and body. I also began to write down my feelings of fear and anguish in a journal. It was hard at first. I worried that someone else would discover my insecurities. So, eventually I threw away or burned most of my writings. But I felt much relief from having said it to myself and releasing it in flames to the universe!

(Years later I would learn about the Paradoxical Theory of Change. The ability to express what you fear creates a favorable condition for it to recede. Who knew?)

Midway through my career, the stakes for my fears grew bigger. I was the spokesperson for one of our nation's Governors. It was an inspiring job that allowed me to travel the world meeting nearly every person I ever dreamed of meeting. That was the positive.

The downside was that I was responsible for relaying to the news media what the Governor thought, planned, did and said. One mistake or misinterpretation and I could cause him trouble and even land on the front pages of newspapers or evening newscasts. It was exhilarating – yet terrifying – work for a 30-something young woman.

In that job, there were many fearful, and even potentially life-threatening moments and crises for the people in our state and for us: death threats to the Governor, tornadoes, floods, droughts, a savings and loan crisis in which thousands of people stormed the Statehouse threatening the lives of the inhabitants (us!)

Yes, one slip of the tongue and I could be toast. (Fortunately, the Governor I worked for was rather forgiving. Once I teasingly questioned why a national group of "swingers" would choose a city as seemingly boring as Akron, Ohio to hold their convention in. My comments ended up in print! Akron's mayor called for my resignation. I had to apologize to him and to the U.S. Congressman representing the district. Ouch.)

I needed to find ways to cope with the scary pit in my stomach almost daily from such episodes. So, before I left home each morning, I spent a few minutes reading the inspiring words of others – even if it made me late for work. In particular, I read the works of political figures: Abraham Lincoln, Teddy and Franklin Roosevelt, Dr. Martin Luther King Jr., Mario Cuomo and Gloria Steinem.

I took comfort that if Abraham Lincoln struggled with fear then I was in great company! I read his words over and over:

"It often requires more courage to dare to do right than to *fear* to do wrong."

Dr. King's *Strength To Love* and "Letter From Birmingham Jail" were well worn by the time I had them practically memorized. His urging to "cultivate a tough mind and lead with a tender heart" spoke to my very soul and gave me resolve.

Diaries of Mario M. Cuomo was also a lifeline to calm myself. That the great Governor of New York Mario Cuomo, a gifted contemporary politician, was up in the early mornings too and writing about his fears, doubts, and the challenges of his hard-pressed, enterprising immigrant family gave me perspective.

And, because I spoke to Governor Cuomo on occasion at meetings, his vulnerable diary entries were all the more poignant and comforting to me because he was pretty big and tough on the outside!

When Gloria Steinem shared in *Outrageous Acts and Everyday Rebellions* her almost pathological fear of public speaking and yet accomplished what she did, she gave me strength and hope.

During my political years, I also began attending church to quell fears and achieve peace of mind. On those Sundays, I learned to be quiet and allow the music and teachings to melt away the week's fears and anxieties. The author is unknown, but this saying reflected my thoughts at the time: "Feed your faith and your fears will starve to death."

I also bought my first self-help audiotape and discovered yet another way to relax away fear. In my time-starved world, I listened to the tape driving to work. I would arrive at the office feeling calm and confident.

It worked like a charm until one day I happened to read the instructions on the tape's cover. I was hypnotizing myself and under no circumstance should I simultaneously listen and drive!

*   *   *   *   *   *   *

Years passed.

And, just when I rarely felt much fear anymore, something unbelievably horrifying happened.

The events of September 11, 2001 terrified many of us in a way we'd never imagined. My husband Rob and I were on Martha's Vineyard and scheduled to fly to Florida through LaGuardia Airport in New York on the night of September 10, 2001.

Our small plane taxied to the runway and then sat idle until the pilot announced the plane would not be leaving Martha's Vineyard because of mechanical problems. There was an odd energy in the air.

We rebooked ourselves through Boston and Charlotte, NC, bypassing New York City, to get to Florida.

We made it no farther than Charlotte that night where we stayed in a hotel in an industrial park near the airport. In the morning, like you, we watched in horror the collapse of the Twin Towers.

Almost always, I traveled with my inspiring, well-worn prayer book *Illuminata* by Marianne Williamson. 9/11 was the one time I hadn't. I felt utterly at loose ends without familiar words of comfort.

After hours of watching the events unfold on television in the hotel lobby with other stunned guests, Rob and I stepped outside for fresh air. It seemed as if the world were coming to an end.

Wandering aimlessly (and me fearfully) in the office park, Rob and I came upon a small, independent bookstore. The very first book I pulled from the self-help shelf was *When The World Breaks Your Heart – Spiritual Ways of Living With Tragedy* by Gregory S. Clapper. Dr. Clapper was a National Guard chaplain who wrote about his experience with those injured and dying after an airplane crash in Sioux City, Iowa in 1989.

The world *had* broken my heart on that grave day. And, the book miraculously provided solace and comforted my fears when I read how others had survived calamity.

When Rob entered my life, I learned and added a whole new treasure chest of techniques to combat fear. One unconventional method in particular helped me through 9/11 and the aftermath that for me included panic attacks on airplanes and driving over bridges.

Did you know that your index fingers are called your "fear fingers?" That's based on Jin Shin Jyutsu, an ancient Japanese healing art and modality of self-healing.

By gently holding your index finger one at a time for several minutes, your fear may fade. For months after 9/11, I held my index fingers and calmed myself. Try it next time you are nervous or fearful in a meeting or unsettling encounter. No one will even notice you are holding your "fear" finger as you become more and more confident!

Today, fear cannot stop me. While I have no way to know your exact struggle with fear, I do know that your gifts, strengths and talents are unique to the world. If fear keeps you from expressing your whole being and full potential, do you realize what a tragic loss that is to our world?

May you always have the skills, techniques and methods that feel right to you to stand tall, face your fears and walk right through them.

*   *   *   *   *   *   *

Debbie Phillips is a pioneer in the field of life and executive coaching and the founder of Women on Fire™. She is known for her work transforming women's lives.

She is the author of *Women on Fire: 20 Inspiring Women Share Their Life Secrets (and Save You Years of Struggle!)* and co-executive producer of the film *Inspire Me!*

Debbie also created and co-developed Vision Day®, the strategic planning program for your life and work, with her husband Rob Berkley, an executive coach and business producer. They live with their big white cat Wilber on Martha's Vineyard, Mass. and in Naples, Fla. You can reach her at www.DebbiePhillips.com

CODE BLUE
Howard Kay

"Nothing in life is to be feared. It is only to be understood."
– Marie Curie

December 7, 2008: It all started with the dizziness. I felt like I had just stepped off a carousel but left my brain on the ride. Closing my eyes didn't help. Lying down didn't help. I didn't understand it. That's when the first inklings of fear crept in.

My chest was burning. Strangely enough, that lessened the fear. The burning sensation felt a lot like acid reflux—I'd had that before so I knew what to do. But none of my usual remedies worked and I realized my symptoms were warning signs. I knew I had to get to a hospital.

In the emergency room I lay on the table in the full grip of fear. I didn't know what was going on and that made it all worse. I waited for almost an hour. Then came the words that struck me down cold:

"Code Blue! Code Blue!"

Code Blue is an active heart attack in progress. I didn't know whether or not I would live. I didn't know what the heart attack was doing to me. As people rushed around me I felt utterly powerless. I'd never felt so scared in my whole life.

Then the doors swung open and a doctor came in. Sure, the room was already full of people tending to me, but I could tell he was different, that he would have the answers I so desperately needed. I know this might sound silly, but in that moment, to me, that doctor was like a knight in shining armor. He said exactly what I needed to hear. He said I was in the right place at the right time.

He went to work. All the resources in the room went toward stopping what was going on in my chest. They put a stent in and everything was fine. That was the end of the heart attack.

The X-rays they showed me later revealed that the main artery of my heart had been 100 percent blocked. The images were shocking, to be sure, but I didn't have the common fear of many heart attack victims, the fear of having another one. I had already moved on. I wanted to know what to do next.

You see I've done a lot of personal development work that had already changed the way I view fear. I've studied with Jack Canfield and studied the power of positive prayer. I've watched the movie *The Secret* many times and read the Law of Attraction works of Esther and Jerry Hicks. I know that if you fear something, if you put negative thoughts in your head, you are inviting that negative thing to happen.

Everyday I make it a point to remove bad thoughts from my mind and replace them with good thoughts. That's how I am, that's how I live.

But my heart attack showed me another way that fear can touch me. The worst I felt was when I lay on that table not knowing. The moment the doctor came in and I knew what was going on and how it would be taken care of, I was fine. That's when I came to understand: ignorance causes fear.

I feared the unknown.

So I threw myself into learning about what would happen next for me. What would I have to do to recover? What was the process? I didn't pay attention to doctors before, but they quickly became my role models. They still have more information than most people. Doctors know what's going on.

This was crucial because, as it turned out, the recovery process was really about doing what the doctors say and monitoring myself closely. It's amazing how easy it is to deal with a heart condition once you know you have it.

I began to study what affects the heart and what doesn't. I began to pay more attention to what I put into my body: less salt, less cheese, less bread. I began to exercise more. I scheduled regular check-ups with my doctor.

Am I glad that I had a heart attack? No. But I am grateful that it showed me this missing piece of my personal development. It's like it showed me a muscle other than my heart that needed strengthening. If I ever feel fear like that again, I'll know what will help me conquer it: knowledge, answers and all the empowerment that comes with having a clear plan of action.

* * * * * * *

Howard Kay, CPA is known as "America's Wellness Coach". He's author of the upcoming book, *You Were Born Healthy: The 7 Essentials For Lifelong Health & Wellness.* You can get a head start on shifting your awareness toward health, wealth, and abundance by going to www. YouWereBornHealthyBook.com to receive your free copy of his companion e-book, *You Were Born Healthy: Quotes & Inspiration for Lifelong Health & Wellness.*

Sailing Past Fear to Discover Flow
Jeneth Blackert

You are standing on railroad tracks when you begin to feel the vibration from the train on the metal rails. You consider running home. Then you hear the clatter of the rails from the oncoming train, the train horn, and your heart starts to race, your body starts to shake and as you turn to run you are suddenly struck with terror. You begin to sweat and then suddenly you realize the train wasn't going to hit, but just pass you by. You are still alive, but you have broken through to a whole new level of awareness and reality.

What is Fear?

The fear we are talking about is not danger. There is no danger to you. However, fear can feel almost as strong as being hit by a steam train in the emotional realm of our existence.

Fear shows up when you halt, stop, feel stuck and even procrastinate. Maybe you have found that something is holding you back but you aren't sure what. Or maybe you are unsure about what to do next? Or maybe suddenly you feel like you hit a wall.

Understanding Your Emotional Waves

I find emotions are best described as ocean waves. It rolls in fast, overwhelms you and takes you down. If you were to fight against it you may drown, but once you allow yourself to surface you catch your next breath and feel peace.

Like ocean waves, emotions roll in and roll out with force and when we understand this we can experience emotions as an incredible opportunity for growth! When we observe the emotional realm, we learn how to observe our reactions and adjust to make fear our friend. And that allows us to be present with fear instead of running for our known safe house. The emotion of fear is an incredible growth tool.

Let's take a deeper look.

How Do You Navigate Through The Lake of Fear?

As you may know your brain loves to hold to the things from past life experiences that are no longer helping you. When you are born your mind was completely open to all experiences equally. You didn't have any preconceived notions! You gave your best in each moment and didn't have any expectations about what might happen in the future. But something happened as we became older. We began to collect every single experience, some that caused us to quit, some that fueled us to do things differently and some that caused us to try to predict the future.

When we try to predict the future based on past experiences, we play an imaginary game that often ends up feeling like fear. You imagine seeing and feeling the oncoming fear train. The train hasn't reached you – it's always in the future. Imagine for a moment what your life would be like if you could imagine seeing only the best possible outcome of everything?

The key to wealth in all areas of your life is to refuse to focus on things that cause you fear, and to eliminate fear from your life. Some clients have said to me, "How can I NOT focus on fear? There is evidence from my past experiences." My answer to them is that you make a *DECISION* not to indulge the thought or emotion.

And the bigger question… if you don't take action fearlessly, are you captive to your imaginary fear and conditioned mind?

Let's look at how to handle the emotion of fear.

How to Handle the Emotion of Fear: A 5-Step Process

Fear is a part of being alive, but many of us don't like to admit we even have it. The first step to handling fear is fully accepting it as a part of you and identifying how it shows up in your life.

Step 1: What's The Next Step?

Have you ever been mountain biking? If you were to look up at the vertical grade of the mountain, your brain would engage, you may feel fear and you wouldn't be able to ride up the mountain. However, when you put the bike in the easiest gear and focus on the next spot of earth you are going to cover, you don't feel as overwhelmed by the fear of the vertical grade. The vision is to get to the top of the mountain but the focus must be on the next step (or push on the pedal). I suggest you start releasing the emotion of fear by taking a deep breath and asking the simple question, "What's my next step towards my vision?"

Step 2: Create a Fear Thought Statement

Start with a journal. On the first page, ask these questions.

How does fear show up for me? What actions terrify me? Acknowledge these thoughts.

What's the complete thought that precedes my fearful emotion?

What are you afraid of? Write it all down starting with "I am afraid _____"

How would you complete this sentence? "I'm afraid if _____ then _____." For example, "I'm afraid if I really step into growing a business then I won't be accepted." "I'm afraid if I invest money into my business then it won't come back to me."

Now, take a moment to recognize the "real" fear emotion. In the example, "I'm afraid if I really step into growing a business then I won't be accepted." Are you afraid to really grow your business or are you afraid you won't be accepted? Which has the biggest emotional impact on you? In this case, you are afraid of not being accepted.

Step 3: Acknowledgment for This Awareness

Now, take a deep breath and honestly thank your subconscious mind. Feel the gratitude! Thank yourself by acknowledging and accepting this thought. Remember, your subconscious mind is just doing what it was programmed to do, acting on what it has observed through life experiences. So when we acknowledge our conscious thoughts and subconscious emotions, we honestly accept ourselves. This in turn causes resistance and denial to be dropped.

Step 4: Discover the Truth Answer these questions.

Is this thought true?

Is this thought true for all mankind?

How do I know this is a true statement?

Step 5: Create a Counter Statement: Start with, "The truth is _____."

5-Step Process Example: Overcoming the Fear of Losing Money

As a wealth attraction mentor for entrepreneurs, I work a lot with clients eager to overcome the fear of not having enough money and losing money. There seems to be a lot of fear wrapped up with spending money as a business investment. Internally they feel strangled. They start to sweat and cannot breathe. They're holding on to their money so tightly that money has difficulty flowing in and out of their life. They feel trapped and always tell themselves that don't have the money! And, get this, oftentimes they have plenty of money in accounts, but they have told themselves they cannot touch it! That is their security blanket.

Let's put it through the 5-Step Process:

Step 1: What's the Next Step?

I invest in ___ for my business.

Step 2: Create a Fear Thought Statement

"I'm afraid if I invest in this ___ then I will lose money."

Step 3: Acknowledgment for this Awareness

I'm afraid I'll lose money

Step 4: Discover the Truth

Is this thought true? *(Money is energy. It's used to represent value and worth you give and receive. In other words, it's products and services bought and sold and I don't know what this investment will do exactly for the future of my business. I can only make the best decision – right now.)*

Is this thought true for all mankind? *(No)*

How do I know this is not a true statement? *(People haven't always lost money when they invested in this business)*

Step 5: Create a Counter Statement Start with, "The truth is people invest in their businesses all the time and don't lose every single cent."

Embrace Your Power to Be Unstoppable

Once you take back your power over your emotions, you'll find you will feel more powerful and become unstoppable. This is because you are giving full attention to the present moment and holding the vision for a greater future. You may be quite surprised to find how easy it is once you implement these simple step-by-step processes.

*　　*　　*　　*　　*　　*　　*

Jeneth Blackert (aka Attraction Diva) is an author, a speaker, and an intuitive business coach. She has personally taught hundreds of individuals her unique principles and approach to massive success. Her principle system, The Wealth Flow System, is based on time-honored universal wisdom. Jeneth is the author of several books and programs including *Seven Dragons: A Guide to a Limitless Mind, Simple Marketing* and the upcoming *Discover Your Inner Strengths. Discover Your Inner Strengths* is co-authored with Stephen Covey and Ken Blanchard.

To learn more about Jeneth and how to find your flow to wealth creation, download your free 70-minute audio at: http://www.beingwealth.com

Feeling Things Fully
Andrea J. Lee

"You're fired!"

"You've been served."

"Keep going like this, and you'll need another surgery."

"Your brother may go to jail."

"Honey, the check bounced again…"

In a book about fear, this may be the most unexpected message you'll hear, so I'll cut to the chase.

In the most challenging of times, when fear starts bubbling up, I think it's important to let that fear boil over, and sometimes allow yourself to feel – with excruciating sensitivity - even more afraid than the situation warrants.

Over the years, I've come to think of fear as a good thing, sometimes even a great thing. And as much as I can, the way I handle it is to…

Treat fear like a super vitamin

Consciously taking a little Vitamin F on a regular basis, I've discovered it makes me much more ready to handle what life brings.

Turning away from fear is, in my book, what we do when we don't know what to do, whereas running *into* fear and feeling it fully is where the answers are!

One thing is for sure - when fear is present, it's difficult to ignore. It's like a homing beacon for your heart, making it beat fast; an emotional divining rod that heightens your awareness, a magnet that draws your attention.

Given that, my next question to you is simple. Why? Why do you think fear has this effect?

For what reason does fear exist?

In a natural environment, the merits of fear are much clearer to spot. You see a predator and you get afraid. The fear makes you run. Running saves your life.

In a city, at your desk, in the comfort of your bathrobe and slippers, fear that grips you from the inside out, with no predator in sight, is more confusing and difficult to decipher.

What is this fear for? What a nuisance! If only this roiling feeling would go away. Wait a sec, maybe if I ignore it, it will.

And, that's what most of us do. We ignore it, rather than use it as the navigation tool for life that it is.

Using fear as a tool

Have you ever wondered what it would be like if the human body came with a dashboard, like in a car?

What if you could tell when you're hungry when the gauge on your stomach started to get near empty?

If you got a head's up that you would be tired in an hour based on the light going off on the oil tank?

Even better, this dashboard should come with stickers that reminded us when regular maintenance needed to be done on teeth, eyes, ears and nose.

But wait! Maybe we do have a dashboard of sorts, one that gives us information about many things, if only we pay attention to it.

The breath, whether it's rapid, shallow, measured, deep or stopped, tells us a lot, for starters.

The eyes, when red, tearing, squinting or rolled back into our head, also tell us a lot, wouldn't you agree?

What about an emotion such as fear, with its attendant rapid heartbeat, adrenalin rush, churning stomach and hair, standing up on the back of our neck or arms?

Fear is a window into data. It's a measuring tool, as surely as the gas gauge in your car. But it's a useless tool if you don't pay attention to it. Your gas dial can blink at you for all its worth and you'll still end up on the side of the road if you're oblivious to it.

How can you feel fear more fully?

In my own experiences of fear, such as the scenarios at the beginning of this chapter, I've evolved a personal set of three things to do. These help me feel fear fully whenever it arises and bit by bit, allows me to use it as a tool for navigating life.

1. Pixelate.

Do you remember the old computer monitors with their green font on black background, and how poor the image quality was, because of the relatively few pixels involved? Today, with the advent of high-definition TV screens, the number of pixels per square inch has increased considerably, and our picture quality has followed suit.

To pixelate is my term for actively increasing the sensitivity of something by increasing the number of pixels on whatever it is. When it comes to fear, how can you increase your sensitivity? Slow down, for starters, and explore each pixel of your fear as if it were a tangible thing. Take notice of everything as if fascinated by it, and in so doing become capable of sensing more data about your fear.

If you continue calmly doing this, at a certain point you may notice yourself relaxing. Keep noticing, pixelating even further if you can. Becoming immersed in the details of the feeling of fear allows you to feel it completely and thoroughly. This may be surprisingly freeing for you, and is a process you can repeat at any time.

2. Enjoy.

It may sound paradoxical to say, "Enjoy your fear" but it's a useful exercise nonetheless. Like all emotions, fear is a state of energy. Energy can pool and stagnate, or it can be put towards something productive.

As you learn to pixelate, you may come to realize that certain kinds of fear actually enhance your senses. Like a dial on a television, fear can sharpen how things look. When you're calmly fearful, you may notice colors seem brighter and sounds become clearer. Your sense of energy soars.

When compared to apathy or exhaustion, for example, there is something in this state to enjoy!

In an alert yet calm state of fear, I can find a lot to appreciate about life. Like salt on your favorite meal, fear can put the flavor into life. I can't imagine life without it.

3. Energize.

Speaking of imagination, a third thing I do with the strong emotions such as fear is turning them into fuel. Coal and oil on our planet are limited resources and by all accounts, slowly running out. Yet everywhere we look, we can see human beings, and within us we have an unlimited amount of emotion.

Would it be useful for more of us to think of fear as fuel? What productive activity can we use that fuel for? How might we hook up that energy to our current project, perhaps something that we're stuck on that needs oomph?

I often imagine how great it would be if we could connect the fitness centers in the world to a giant windmill, and channel the treadmill-walking, bicycle-pedaling, weight-lifting energy into something that produced food. What if we could do that same thing with our emotions like fear?

I say we can, and that it's only a matter of linking fear with your life's work in your mind. So start small. When you have pixelated, begun feeling your feelings fully, started to enjoy those sensations, and now have excess energy waiting inside you, pick something to do! Scrub those dirty pots and pans. Tackle a to-do list item. Go to the park with the kids.

A little at a time, this habit of pixelating, enjoying and energizing can become a useful new habit, and you'll begin to understand how to use fear as a tool to navigate life.

Fear treated as the enemy will grow to be the enemy
Over the years, I've coached artists, entrepreneurs and lawyers. I've

worked with people on the poverty line and people who are millionaires many times over. The one thing I see in common among all of them is that unchecked, their fear haunts them in the form of bad health.

Like the beach ball that pops back up out of the water after you shove it down, when you try to bury fear, it finds a way to spring up full force, and sometimes, reach up and grab you by the throat.

It happened to me. Two years ago I underwent a significant abdominal surgery for something no one could explain. What should have been a quick surgery took nearly 3 hours. Two pounds of my body were removed, and I spent 5 days in the hospital.

I know that suppressing fear was a big part of the reason this happened: fear of not being good enough for a high-achieving, immigrant family; fear of marrying an outsider and losing my ethnic community; fear of not earning enough money. Of course there was also the fear of letting people down.

All of these things have been part of my life, and I can't imagine they won't continue. Which is why I left the hospital determined to find another relationship with fear.

If suppressing it backfires, how about embracing it?

If ignoring fear doesn't work, how about seeking it out and observing it?

These days, I'm clear that the very biggest fears in my life have shaped it, much as a river carves out the banks of a delta. And I'm curious what shapes it will bring.

The fiercest fear of all

Still, I continue to struggle with what I consider to be the greatest fear of all, for all of us.

It's the fear of saying goodbye. Dying. Not using my life well.

I once heard a theory about divorce. That people subconsciously don't commit fully to their relationships because if they do, one day they'll have to say goodbye to that person, or that person will have to say goodbye to them.

The fear of saying goodbye too soon, with unfinished life work, more living left to do, more loving to express, is a natural fear that is ferocious in its power. It's a gift in dirty paper.

If we can focus on the tiny pixels of that fear, even just a little each day, and enjoy how that energizes us for the work and loving we have in front of us, I think we're on the right track.

In the heat of your fear, I hope you'll remember that learning is what happens only when we really don't know what to do. Whatever your way of addressing fear – in your business or with your family – may this be the start of your adventure to feeling your feelings fully, and letting fear be a navigation tool in your life.

*   *   *   *   *   *   *

Andrea J. Lee is a visionary business and life coach who guides exceptional clients to the success they seek, while championing them to become more and more uniquely themselves. Her coaching is said to be a blend of tenderness and bite unlike any other, and one of her most celebrated abilities is coining metaphors that melt your biggest blocks.

She is the author of *Money, Meaning and Beyond: 27 Unexpected Ways To Create What Really Matters, For Business Owners* and *Pink Spoon Marketing*. To read more about Andrea and her views on how to achieve what you want in life including pixelating your fear, visit www.MyThoughtPartners.com.

How to Handle Fear…
In Business

Confronting Your Fears
Donald J. Trump

Fear defeats more people than any other thing in the world.
–Ralph Waldo Emerson

To ask the right question is already half the solution of a problem.
–Carl Jung

Recently, an interviewer asked me what my greatest fears were. I said I didn't have any. He seemed surprised, but this is how I see it: If you label something as a fear, then it creates fear when sometimes it's not a fear but a concern. For example, I know just as well as everyone else that New York City experienced a major terrorist attack and the thought of that is a concern for all of us, because it affects all of us. It's happened in many places, so it's a worldwide concern. But if we let it become a firmly rooted fear, the terrorists will have won.

The same applies to business. Do you fear owning a business? Translate that for yourself as asking: Are you concerned about owning a business yourself? Why? What specifically are those concerns? It's much easier to break down a concern than it is a fear. Fear creates a block that will only hinder your creative thinking. Objectivity will remove that block and allow for creative ideas to flow.

An antidote to fear is as simple as problem solving. Whether you have investing, estate planning, or running a business on your mind, or all of those things, they can be broken down into units of thought and dealt with in an orderly manner. It's a bit like a jigsaw puzzle—you need to find the right place for each piece of the puzzle until the whole is apparent.

When I began to construct Trump Tower, for example, I had several things in mind that I knew I wanted. I wanted a certain kind of marble called Breccia Perniche, which was expensive, beautiful, and rare. It was also irregular and had white spots and white veins, which bothered me, so I went to the quarry itself and marked off the best slabs with black tape. Action turned this concern into a problem solved. I got exactly the marble pieces I wanted, and sitting around worrying about whether those pieces would be right or wrong was getting me nowhere. As a result of deciding to go to the quarry myself, the pieces of this puzzle fell into place and the finished product was perfect.

Know that if you want to own your own business, you will be doing a lot of the work yourself. That's just the way it is. It isn't all about giving orders or having other people do the legwork or brainwork for you. That comes into the picture, but you should always be ready to go at it yourself. If that idea bothers you, maybe you'd be better off being an employee. If responsibility comes naturally to you, or if you enjoy that challenge, owning your own business is a good fit.

Fear has a way of making things bigger than they are. There's an old German proverb to the effect that "fear makes the wolf bigger than he is," and that is true. But the opposite of fear is faith, which is one reason you've got to believe in yourself and see yourself as victorious. You will know you are capable of dealing with any discouragements, bullies, or problems along the way.

When I was faced with some huge debts in the early 1990s, it was widely reported that I was finished, done for, gone. Looking at the numbers alone made that seem clear to the media. However, I never believed I was finished. I simply saw that situation as a problem I had to solve and went about doing that. I'm not saying it was easy, because it wasn't. It was a big problem. But I refused to give in to fear or to believe what was being said about my so-called demise. I came back to become more successful than I ever was, and that's why I believe business is very much about problem solving. If you can learn to deal with and solve problems, you will have a much bigger margin for success.

Do not allow fear to settle into place in any part of your life. It is a defeating attitude and a negative emotion. Recognize and zap it immediately. Replace it with a problem-solving attitude, faith in yourself, and hard work. Put that formula into working order for yourself and you'll be dealing from a position of power, not fear. That's winning.

*   *   *   *   *   *   *

Donald J. Trump is the Chairman and President of The Trump Organization. He is the preeminent developer of quality real estate around the world, making the Trump brand synonymous with the gold standard. His commitment to excellence extends from his real estate holdings to the entertainment industry. As the star and co-producer of the NBC hit series *The Apprentice*, to his award-winning golf courses and skyscrapers, his business acumen is unparalleled. His Trump Tower on Fifth Avenue has become one of the most famous landmark buildings in New York City, and his Trump International Hotel & Tower in New York City has received the coveted Mobil Five-Star Award. He is the archetypal businessman—a deal maker without peer and an ardent philanthropist.

The Leap Over Fear
Darren West

In 2001 while working for a Fortune 500 Company I experienced my first and last layoff along with numerous other employees being downsized throughout the northwestern region of the United States.

The four to five months I spent without any income trying to support my wife and three children at the time was a stressful period for me. While grieving the end of my well-paying sales career I realized I had to step-up, take control, and continue to move forward. Now, looking back I can see it was one of the best times of my life – because I put my fear aside. When everything seems like life has come crashing down around you, it would be so easy to let fear consume your whole being. It's in those times of adversity that you must rely on the way you have preprogrammed yourself to handle adversity and fear. Do not permit your fear, emotions, or apprehensions to overpower your thoughts, feelings, or actions.

For me it required a mental shift, a change in direction. I began building support for change, and demonstrating by approach: "Optimism is the faith that leads to achievement – Helen Keller." Honing in on my creative juices and systematically assessing the Health Care industry, I found a need within the industry to put all my efforts towards. While working for a local Sleep Institute at night, I spent my days with my partner John Holman, combining our efforts towards the creation, organization, and maintaining of Caring Hearts Senior Care. Our mission was and is to help seniors to maintain their independence and age gracefully within their own home setting by providing assistance with activities of daily living.

Over the years, through challenges and triumphs, we have built two Assisted Living Facilities that complement our in-home business. Within the Assisted Living Facilities our goal is to enhance our residents' quality of life by providing a home-like setting that fosters independence, dignity, and choice in a safe, loving, and caring atmosphere.

As we all know, through the various walks of life, people will come up against life's challenges as I did whether due to layoffs, changing market trends, or the economy. I would like to encourage each and every person to treat life's challenges and fears as stepping-stones. Everything you've learned up to this point in life will aid you in your future successes.

Success has come to me over the years for the most part without a big price. This was only possible after I was able to realize how the bondage of fear was holding me back. With the development and expansion of three companies and one in the planning, I've been able to develop 6 steps on how to overcome fear and use these steps as tools to approach risk and take smart-quality steps towards big opportunities. I would like to pass them on to you.

1. Pre-program yourself to be an achiever.
2. Act with consistency.
3. Have mentors.
4. Push yourself, but always look for a soft landing.

5. Be both a teacher and a student.

6. Do acts of service.

1. <u>Pre-program yourself to be an achiever.</u> I'm a big believer that we need to put twice as much effort towards positive reinforcement of our own self-confidence to help wash out the daily flow of negativity. I'm able to focus on daily tasks and brainstorm new opportunities best after I've spent time to recharge my battery through motivational self-help books and audios. As I learn and gain knowledge, I'm realizing a key factor to turning that knowledge into power is to act on that newfound knowledge. Write your thoughts and recently gained enlightenment down in a rough draft format, just to get the initial idea down on paper. Then review and improve upon the draft until the change you visualized is realized. My personal preference is to surround myself with a huge variety of content. One of my favorite resources is *Success* Magazine and *Success* book summaries. Both have a wide variety of topics and many of my favorite mentors frequently grace the pages of these publications.

2. <u>Act with Consistency.</u> Fear leads to procrastination, which is an enemy of action. **Action** eliminates fear. Looking back on my success, it has been the small action steps taken on a daily basis with consistency that has helped with each new launch of development. As long as you are taking those daily action steps towards your goals you are moving forward. Another distraction and discomforting feeling is a lack of consistency. Lack of consistency is one of the main factors why individuals or new start-ups don't succeed. Example: when starting a new venture, competition will be a factor. It's also evident that most competitors are inconsistent, hot and cold. I love the analogy that

Brian Tracy uses about a plan getting off the ground. "It takes more fuel (energy) to get the plane going 80 mph on the ground than it does for the plane to cruise at 400 mph in the air."

So remember one of the most important items when going "head to head" with your competitors is **consistency**. It's never about how you start; it's always about how you continue that counts.

3. Have Mentors. If you don't already have a mentor, get one! This will always be your sure way of extinguishing fear and your shortest route to success. With each new business venture we have had a mentor. It will always be more cost effective, quicker, and less painful when you enlist the aid of your mentor's experience, abilities, and know-how. A good mentor will help overcome any fear of the change you are looking for. "Many of our fears are tissue-paper thin, and a single courageous step would carry us clear through them" – Brendon Francis [Behan]

4. Push yourself, but always look for a soft landing. Another good way to beat fear is to have a clear vision of how you're going to get from point A to point B with as few bumps and bruises as possible.

A good example of this is my oldest son Mathew. He loves to ski and it's clear he has natural talent. He has entered several slope style competitions in and around Utah and Idaho. It's clear to him if you want to impress the judges you have to flip and twist on as many as 5 or 6 jumps down the ski course. To stay competitive Mat has been continuing to train during the summer at the Olympic water ramps in Park City, Utah.

Within just a few trips to the water ramps my son has perfected and has passed off on tricks that I would not have dreamed of trying on snow.

Not only does my son have the benefit of landing in water, but landing in lots and lots of bubbles coming up through the water that soften his landing. Watching him brings back my own memories as a young skier. My friends and I would push each other to try different tricks, but it took many seasons to eventually be able to do a single back flip, and then a double-back flip on some really hard landings.

In the last several years many sports have progressed at lightning speed. Eight years ago no one would have thought it would be possible to take a 250-pound motorcycle and do a double back flip off of a 40-foot jump and land it perfectly. Thanks to people like Travis Pastrona who was instrumental in finding a way to soften their landings, by constructing foam pits the size of large swimming pools, dirt bike riders have a safer and better way to practice landing those extreme tricks.

Individually we can learn from some of today's top athletes and mentors that the fear of something new is only the fear of the unknown, and the fear of what you will become in the process. Landing in water or a pool of foam only helps put the mind at ease. You still have to trust your abilities and training enough to eventually "jump in". And jumping in with the help of a good coach or mentor, the landing can and should be painless.

5. <u>Be both a teacher and a student</u>. When learning something new, first be a good student. Then when you have the opportunity to teach what you have learned, this is when you will truly master that new discipline. I've found the most successful people never lose sight of the constant need for growth and learning. My particular choice of profession, the Health Care Industry, has served me well. I've learned vast amounts of practical and insightful life lessons from all kinds of mentors from all walks of life.

6. <u>Do acts of service</u>. The last point that is a sure way to wipe out any remaining fear is to give back through service. Service allows you to let your ego go, and to remember it's not all about how much you accomplish or accumulate in this life. Fear can make us turn inward and focus too much on ourselves. It's important to focus on others, not thinking less of ourselves, but thinking of ourselves *less*. Therein dwells the secret that so many others have written about and experienced for themselves. As you get lost in the service of others, success is bound to follow. Fear is more than an emotion to me. I know from personal experience that fear is a robber of one's potential. And when you feel any part of fear creeping into your state of mind, focus on one or more of these 6 points with intensity so that fear won't have a negative effect in your life. Doing so was a big lesson I had to learn that has helped me in all aspects of my life, and I hope it helps you too.

* * * * * * *

Darren West is an author, speaker, business owner, coach, and is the President/CEO, co-founder/owner of Caring Hearts Senior Care. He brings over 20 years of experience in working within the health care industry. Owning and running three companies, he specializes in coaching small businesses with growth strategies, and those wishing to break into the demanding health care market with turnkey business models. You can contact Darren at Darren@myseniorcarestrategies.com or find him on the Web at: http://www.myseniorcarestrategies.com http://www.caringheartsseniorcare.com

Collaboration:
The Key to Conquering Fear
Sandie Glass

*F*ear…just saying the word out loud has a horrible, negative vibe to it. Fear is the emotional condition that triggers a "fight or flight" response caused by many limiting thoughts and beliefs. It has been my experience over the years that the majority of people prefer to deal with *fear* by simply avoiding it by coming up with a variety of excuses like "I don't want to do that anyway." But what many don't understand is that they are missing out on one of the most powerful emotions that can lead to both personal and business growth and success.

Winston Churchill has been quoted as saying "Fear is a reaction. Courage is a decision." But it leads us to believe that we are to overcome fear alone. Imagine the energy it would take for you, all alone, to confront fear head-on—to stay focused, to have the conviction to push yourself out of your comfort zone and through your fear.

I believe it is smarter and a lot less painful to not go it alone. Put a team together to help you tackle what you fear—friends, family members, co-workers, or you could join an organization. If you are afraid of public speaking, for instance, but know this is something that you really want to do, then find someone that has experience with public speaking and get their advice on how to get started and overcome any fears you may have.

Truth is, people genuinely enjoy helping others and they would be more than happy to share their experience and expertise with you to help you overcome your fear. You just have to ask.

Fear can make us laugh or make us tremble. Just for a moment, take yourself back to your favorite amusement park with those scary yet awesome rollercoaster rides. Now, be honest… you were probably a bit hesitant to get on a new ride all by yourself, right? But you happened to be with a group of your friends who coaxed and challenged you to get on the ride with them. In fact, without realizing it, they gave you the courage to do it because they were going to be right there with you. You got in line with your friends and experienced the anticipation.

Then you got into the seat and the safety bar locked down around you-- there was no turning back! The ride started, slowly climbing that first 135-foot, heart-stopping drop, then raced wildly up, down, and spiraling as the adrenaline rushed through your veins. And then, before you knew it, it rolled slowly to a stop. You got off the ride and then the reality of what you had just done set in. You began to re-live each wild turn with your friends and the stories escalated with others at school that had not experienced it yet. That was the real prize wasn't it…the "bragging rights" and the feeling of accomplishment?

So what exactly happened at the amusement park? The camaraderie and coaxing of your friends eliminated the intensity of any fear you had. It made something that seemed a challenge to tackle alone, less threatening when shared together. That is the power of collaboration in action.

It's no different when dealing with business challenges, but many managers are so fearful of criticism and failure that they succumb to the "status quo"– doing the same thing over and over again yet expecting a different outcome. Only by putting yourself "out there" and challenging the status quo, will you ever achieve those "bragging rights" which will lead to not only the success of the initiative, but ultimately rocketing yourself up the corporate ladder. It's all part of the risk/reward formula. The more your put yourself out there and take those risks, the more you will get in return for your reward.

Alone we seem to be vulnerable, but with others, we are unstoppable! Collaboration – also called "Group Genius" or "Master Minds"— has been the source of awesome creativity and giant leaps of wealth. The famous author Napoleon Hill devoted 20 years of his life studying the wealthiest, most successful men of his time – Andrew Carnegie, Henry Ford, Thomas Edison, Charles Schwab – to write his book *Think and Grow Rich*. The one thing all these men had in common was surrounding themselves with smart men – even those smarter than themselves – and collaborating on various business problems together. Here's a quick history lesson for you… the creation of the United States of America was based on the collaboration of 56 men who put their lives on the line by signing the Declaration of Independence. Take a moment to think about what those men actually did…if the American Revolution hadn't been successful, it could have meant their deaths by hanging! Talk about handling fear with fierceness and courage!

I have owned an Innovation Consultancy (or Think-tank) called Sandstorm Inc. for over 18 years and I have seen the power of collaboration among team members in relation to brainstorming sessions. Upfront planning (which includes asking the right questions, looking in the right places, putting the right group of minds together and inspiring creative thought) coupled with an optimistic mindset (believing that there are many solutions just waiting to be found), are the most important factors affecting the outcome of these sessions.

Now, you'd think that since our project success with clients is grounded in the power of collaboration, that I would have tapped into this power to advance my own business. Unfortunately, I fell victim to not being able to "see the forest through the trees." When I started Sandstorm Inc., I was a one-person organization, doing all aspects of the everyday business functions. I became part-time bookkeeper, part-time sales, part-time marketing, full-time client services manager, and full-time project leader for all work that came in. I had little time to be a visionary, nor did I have the energy to create new growth strategies for my business. It was overwhelming to say the least. The logic was that you never wanted to turn down work because you never knew when the next project was going to come along. My marketing became non-existent, bookkeeping was done "under fire," and sales became solely repeat customers and word-of-mouth.

It was working for a while, but then things fell apart. Clients moved on to new organizations and new managers hadn't gotten their feet wet yet, nor were they comfortable using their predecessor's supplier. Many wanted to make their own mark on the world and bring in different vendors. So the "project well" dried up and there I sat with no sales. It was a challenging time, but a great wake-up call.

It didn't take me long to figure out that I cannot do it all alone and do it well. Nor is it any fun to do it alone. I wanted to share my "wins" and "bragging rights" with others! I needed to reach out and collaborate with business coaches, sales experts, and have open dialogues with old and new clients to strengthen my service offerings, keep me focused and develop sales and marketing plans for success. I needed to outsource things that weren't my strengths or interest and invest in resources that had the expertise I needed to strengthen my company. In fact, I recently took on a partner in my business, and the change has been phenomenal. Marketing and sales materials seemed to magically happen overnight just by opening myself up to collaborating. We are currently exploring opportunities to partner with organizations that have potential synergy with our business. We are excited about our future, not fearful of failure – all through the power of collaboration!

We believe that we can accomplish any goal if we stay focused and collaborate as a team. I go into every client project recalling the inspirational movie *Apollo 13*. Astronaut Jim Lovell (played by Tom Hanks) radioed Mission Control in Texas about 55 hours into the mission with those fateful words, "Houston, we've had a problem." As Flight Director Gene Kranz (played by Ed Harris) calmed down and brought focus to his co-workers, he told them, "…Failure is not an option!" In a personal interview about the movie, Kranz said, "when bad things happened, we just calmly laid out all the options. We never panicked, and we never gave up on finding a solution."

I personally feel that collaboration is the secret to success for all challenges in this world big and small. Fear alone holds us back from accomplishing the impossible.

*   *   *   *   *   *   *

Sandie Glass is an innovation expert, brand growth strategist, experienced facilitator, trained researcher and visionary. As the "Idea Chick of the Planet", she brings 18 years experience working in the upfront innovation processes. She has helped countless Fortune 500 companies like Procter & Gamble, Disney, Nike, American Express, GlaxoSmithKline and M&M/Mars tap into their creativity to achieve remarkable business solutions for market success. Her extraordinary talents take the "blinders off" to unleash the opportunities necessary to connect with consumers who BUY. You can contact Sandie at:

sandie@sandstormideas.com or on the Web at:

http://www.sandstormideas.com/

http://www.linkedin.com/in/sandieglass

Four Servings of Fear, Please
Debra Arrato

"If I'm not home accepting what I cannot change, I'm probably out changing what I cannot accept."
—Pamela Glasner, author

Many people thought I was nuts. It was 1990 and I had been married for five years and had also worked for a commercial bank for those same five years. I had a cushy job as a bank branch manager and assistant vice president (when it was a respected and coveted position of 9-3, no weekends, and four weeks vacation). Things were good within the bank but I was starting to get the "baby itch." Every time I saw a baby, it would make me want one of my own (and I saw a lot of babies). I knew for certain that I didn't want to use daycare. I wanted to raise my family and this was paramount for me.

The wheels started to turn inside my head. (Imagine a perpetually moving hamster wheel. I'm convinced that's what it looks like on the inside of my cranium). As we had recently become first time homebuyers, my husband and I needed the two incomes from our jobs, which meant I couldn't just leave without replacing my income. So I started looking at other options. There weren't many jobs that would pay my current salary and allow me to work from home.

Fear started to set in. At first, it was fear that what I wanted was out of my control. Yes, I am a hardcore control freak. I'm the kind of person who likes, (no actually needs), to have control. If someone tells me I can't do something, I get a pit in my stomach and then I get mad. I will automatically think of alternate ways to achieve what I want.

You see fear to me is relative. My greatest fear is one of illness or death for me, or someone in my family. And I relate all aspects of my life to this. Illness and death are two things over which I have absolutely no control. Virtually everything else in life can be adjusted, changed and adapted. So if I am presented with a problem, a concern, or an opportunity, I know that if I make a poor decision, the results are not set in stone. Something positive can still present itself. And I look for and expect that "positive."

In this instance, if I wanted a family, I would need money. In order to earn money, I needed a job. Other people controlled jobs. How could I get what I wanted? What would I have to give up or change?

I realized this was a universal problem. How many women wanted to stay at home and raise their families but couldn't afford to? How many women hated rising each morning, dragging their little ones to a daycare facility, and crying all the way to their offices because they knew that they wouldn't see their children again until the evening? That scenario was forefront in my mind and I was going to do everything within my power to avoid it.

After scouring the want ads for weeks, I found one that sounded right up my alley. It described a home-based job with a flexible schedule earning about $200 a night. It turned out to be a direct sales company marketing products primarily to women during short in-home presentations—a party plan business. Being the eternal optimist, I saw only the advantages of the business: flexible hours, excellent income potential and the ability to leave the bank to start a family! But I'm not a complete lunatic—I didn't leave my job the next day. I decided to work a couple of evenings a week to "test the waters." I discovered I enjoyed the business and was actually making some money.

The funny thing was that I realized I didn't need to make the proverbial "million dollars." The goal wasn't to be a millionaire, but to have enough money to be comfortable working from home. After a few months, I started to think seriously about leaving the bank.

That's when the fear of failure set in. My husband was not 100% behind me, so I needed to be completely confident that I could do this. But how could I be completely confident? I was earning less than half my bank income working two nights a week. There were no guarantees and the mortgage had to be paid every month. I contemplated for weeks if I should resign. Looking back, I realize it was actually a process I went through:

** I pictured my current situation and what I didn't like about it.
** I pictured how I wanted the situation to be.
** I made lists.

I am a definite list maker. This is how I analyze a situation. My lists included:

Financial List: How much money did I absolutely HAVE to earn each month? This was figured into how much I could earn each night on average and how many evenings I would have to work in the month to earn the equivalent to my bank income. I also calculated miscellaneous expenses that would be saved, i.e., gas, lunches, and dry cleaning.

Things I Would Lose List: I would lose the security of a "job" with a weekly paycheck. I would lose the normalcy of a 40-hour workweek. I would lose 4 weeks paid vacation. I would lose "status", going from a manager/assistant vice president to the bottom of the totem pole with a new company.

Things I Would Gain List: My income wouldn't be guaranteed, but the opportunity to earn what I needed or even more was possible. No one would decide if I was getting a raise each year or how much it would be. I could win all-expense paid vacations with the new company. There was an opportunity to advance into management. I could work the hours that I wanted.

Worst Case Scenario List: What was the absolute worst thing that could happen if I left the bank? The direct sales business would not be successful and I would not earn the money needed to be able to work from home. I thought to myself, even if the worst happens, *I wouldn't die*. I would adapt and move on.

As soon as I said this to myself, I knew I had made the decision. A huge weight was lifted from my shoulders. I was going to do it and I would do everything possible to be successful. I gave the bank my two weeks notice.

I knew I needed my own space to work from home. I bought a desk and chair from an office supply store, along with an all-in-one phone, fax and copier. But I feel the most important things I bought for my new home-based business were the motivational and inspirational items.

I had tons of motivational books by authors such as Zig Ziglar, Anthony Robbins, Napoleon Hill and my idol, real estate extraordinaire Barbara Corcoran. I had sayings on plaques posted all over the walls. "Nothing is Impossible", "Don't Wait for Your Ship to Come In, Swim Out to It", and "If You Dream It, You Can Do It" greeted me every day. Everywhere I looked, something on my desk or hanging on a wall inspired a positive attitude. If I felt down, I would immediately read a few passages from the quote books and marvel at the fact that my success was in my control. When I didn't want to pick up the phone to make a cold call, I looked at the note that said, "If you don't ask, the answer is NO." It helped me make the calls. I also found that the more you could read about successful people who have already done what you want to do, the better. Success stories will fill you with hope and a feeling that "you can do it too."

Over the next six years, I thoroughly enjoyed the business. Working about three nights a week, I recruited over 400 people and was able to exceed my bank income. I became pregnant about a year and a half after leaving the bank and had a healthy baby girl. I was able to stay at home with the baby during the day and my husband was able to watch her while I was working three nights a week. Seems like the perfect ending to a happy story, right?

But I was starting to get the itch again. Only this time it wasn't the baby itch. We were blessed to have our second child, a healthy son born four years after our daughter, so that itch had definitely been scratched!

I seem to get a new "itch" about every five years or so to start something new. I know it sounds crazy. If you are doing well at something, why rock the boat? For me, I enjoy that feeling of excitement from trying something new. But along with that came that same feeling of fear of failure. What if I fell flat on my face? What would people think if I failed? These were some of the same feelings I had when I was contemplating leaving the bank.

But you know what? I just used my list strategy again—and it worked! It became my go-to system. Over the course of the next fifteen years, I used my list system, eternal optimism and motivational items to help me open three more businesses. On average, I owned them for about five years each. They include a gift basket business, a biweekly mortgage service business and a chocolate fountain rental business.

This may sound cliché, but I have found that no matter what the product, a person can be successful with a positive attitude. Weigh all the options. Make lists of best case and worst-case scenarios. If the worst should happen, what are your options? Can you adapt? Research and surround yourself with inspirational and motivational people, books, and quotes. Remember that nothing is ever really cast in stone. The stones can be altered at any time.

Fear is an emotional response to a threat, and it branches out of the unknown. For example, leaving one's comfort zone can establish fear. However, if the situation is thoroughly researched and analyzed, the onset of fear can be significantly diminished. I live by this.

*   *   *   *   *   *   *

Debra Arrato is a 20-year veteran entrepreneur who has started and grown four profitable home-based businesses. She has created *The Homestyle Entrepreneur's 4 Ways to $50K – FIRE YOUR DAYCARE!* E-Book Series. Each e-Book shows how you can earn $50,000 a year working part time from home. If you would like to learn more about the four businesses and how you can make one work for you, visit www. HomestyleEntrepreneur.com.

What is Your Sum?
The Measure of Success
Dr. Laureen Wishom

It is a recognized maxim that fear is the greatest barrier to achieving goals. Fifteen years ago, I worked 50+ hours a week to ensure great performance in my corporate role. I knew that I wanted to start my own company, but deep within I had a definite fear of failure.

After holding numerous leadership positions during my tenure in corporate America, I realized that I did not want to break the "glass ceiling," and settle for an annual three to five percent increase for the rest of my employment. During the last four years of my corporate career, I followed my intuition and founded Masterpiece Solutions LLC. Subsequently, in 1998, I bid adieu to corporate and began my full-time career as the CEO of Masterpiece Solutions.

As a budding entrepreneur I was well aware of the typical seven stages of a business life cycle and can equate each phase of my fears into one of the seven stages of a typical business life cycle (seed, start-up, growth, established, expansion, decline and exit). I completed the seed stage (financial planning and the development of an elementary business plan) during the last four years of my corporate employment.

Start-up Stage

After leaving the corporate world, I entered the start-up stage. Like most new business owners, I experienced the fear of wondering if I made the right decision. Do I really know enough to run my own company? Can I afford to do this? Have I researched enough? Did I select the right target market? Am I really competent enough? What about this one: Do I possess the necessary business and leadership skills?

One of the things that I did on a daily basis during this stage was to write and to make a daily practice of reading an affirmation, which stated: "I will not fail, but if I do, I'll use the failure as a stepping stone to my next success. I will not let a little thing called fear have dominion in my life."

Here are the building blocks I used to face and combat fear during this stage:
- Find a mentor and become a protégé
- Set aside money to run my household and business (for nine months)
- Allocate money for marketing materials (most new businesses forget to set aside money for marketing expenses)
- Build an extensive Rolodex (advertise by word-of-mouth)
- Network, network, network

Growth Stage

I define these years as developing the competencies to become a successful CEO. I often had to read my affirmation statement five or six times a day to suppress that dreadful feeling called fear. There was so much to do: learning, growing and earning.

In addition to living by my daily affirmation, here are the growing blocks that I implemented during this stage:

- Stay focused on the vision
- Stay connected with like-minded individuals
- Develop a "gratitude attitude"
- Give back more than I receive (become a mentor)
- Gain the knowledge and training needed to be successful
- Generate multiple streams of income
- Read, read, read
- Network, network, network

At this point in my business life cycle, I truly believed that "as high as I reach, I can grow; as far as I see, I can go; as deep as I look, I can see; and as much as I dream, I can be".

Turning Point Stage

This stage is not part of the typical business life cycle, but for me it was a stage that required creative problem solving. Having finally overcome the fear of business failure, I had to face the fear of failing health and I was not sure what lay ahead if my health did not improve. How could I continue to operate my company? So, here is what I did to face my health fears and grow my business at the same time:

- Stop wearing all the hats, use outside resources to assist in crunch times.
- Develop systems and processes for repetitive tasks

- Instead of networking without focus, I began to network in the places where potential clients could be found, and also where I can build high-end relationships
- Develop a prosperity and healthy body mindset
- Walk the faith walk, instead of the fear walk, every moment of the day
- Read inspirational materials
- Each day, write five things I am thankful for in my "Gratitude Journal"
- Exercise daily and schedule time for: 1) self and relaxation, 2) getting healthy, and 3) family and friends

Established and Expansion Stages

This phase of the maturation of Masterpiece Solutions encompasses two stages of the typical business life cycle (established and expansion). It was at this point that I began public speaking in order to gain national recognition. I began questioning whether I was ready, and yes fear told me "You will never be ready", but faith said, "You are ready." I chose to listen to faith and followed these principles:

- Up-level my daily thought process
- Leverage every opportunity
- Close the gap between words and actions
- Network with a purpose
- Think globally and continue to generate multiple streams of income
- Raise the bar at every level (business, personal, and professional)
- Continue to write five things to be thankful for in the

"Gratitude Journal"

- Mentor, mentor, mentor (in 2007 I was the recipient of the *Stevie Award*™ Mentor of the Year)
- Become saturated in the learning process, it allows no time for fear (I attend over twenty teleseminars each month)
- Maintain a protégé status
- Re-invent, re-purpose and re-position
- When fear knocks at your door, send faith to answer

By the way, the remaining stages of the typical business life cycle are "decline" and "exit". I have not yet entered these two stages. They will manifest in the future and I am sure they will have their own unique challenges and engender some initial fears.

I have conquered my fears at every other stage of the business life cycle and I know that when the time comes for these two stages, fear will not win. As part of my preparation for these final stages, I have drafted an exit strategy that will allow me to generate revenue unlike most entrepreneurs who will walk away with little capital.

I want to share my life-long mantra with you and hopefully it will help you as you face your fears: "Maintain a positive attitude, learn to overcome obstacles, become a systems thinker, keep a balance in life, become a teacher and leader, eliminate fear daily and get rid of whatever makes you stop."

For those of you who wish to conquer your fears and to start a business remember the words of Henry Hartman, "Success always comes when preparation meets opportunity."

By realizing that we are the creators of our own reality, we can choose to fear, or we can choose not to fear. So let me close with this thought: You are the sum of the five people with whom you spend the most time. If your five people maintain a "fear mentality"...well, you do the math. "What is your sum?"

*   *   *   *   *   *   *

Dr. Laureen Wishom is a career success and business growth expert, strategist and *solutionist*™. She is the Founder/CEO of Masterpiece Solutions LLC and the Global Association of High-Achieving Women. Her strong interpersonal leadership style has positively influenced the bottom line of many small and mid-size companies.

She is the author of a series of "How To" books on developing your business DNA, customer service, getting noticed, obtaining a corporate board seat, and career development and branding. Her specialty is upleveling female career professionals and catapulting women business owners to their next platform. For more about information about Laureen and her work please visit http://www.masterpiecesolutions.biz; www.gahaw.com; or call 281.584.0348.

How to Handle Fear…
In Career and Money Matters

Fighting Fear With Fear
Caroline Ceniza-Levine

I am an extreme career-changer: classical pianist, banker, management consultant, executive recruiter, actor, life coach, corporate HR director, real estate investor, and entrepreneur. I have worked in different industries doing different jobs. I have worked in big and small companies. I have worked alone, with big groups and leading teams. I have made big changes in my personal and my professional life, in up and in down markets.

However, if you told me early on that the above would describe my career path, I would have dismissed you. I am risk-averse. I don't take chances like starting a business or entering rejection-ridden fields like acting. I'm too afraid to do any of these things I just listed above.

And yet I did. And so can you. I'm still full of fear – that's just how I am. I worry a lot. I imagine the worst. I see half empty glasses everywhere. But I developed strategies, techniques, and tips that enabled me to press on, even with the fear ever present.

As it turns out, these same strategies helped other people, and so I write about them and lead workshops about them, coaching people on how to overcome their own fears. I truly believe we can have everything we really want and are willing to work for. (That's what I think on my best days anyway; on my regular days, I get fearful, lose some time worrying, and then consciously coach myself to move on.)

When I am afraid, I run over the numbers. How much will I make? How much debt will it require? How long will this take? So in one of my biggest career changes to date -- from experienced (and salaried) recruiter to novice (and nomadic) actor -- I tracked my budget for over a year before I made the leap so I knew exactly what I spent (and therefore how much I'd need), and I saved as much of that as I could.

Running the numbers is a way to out-think your fear. Many of my clients don't run any numbers and are afraid of things that don't exist. For example, they assume they need to take a pay cut when research shows they do not. They assume that they can't afford whatever investment they need (e.g., more training, time off to ramp up), when the numbers show they have what they need. Before you assume that something is too expensive or you don't have the time, run the numbers.

The first sign we don't know what we are doing is an obsession with numbers. - Johann Wolfgang von Goethe

That said, I know I need to move on when the numbers come back good and I still can't act. The numbers might reveal a possible plan of action, but they don't force you to act. For this, I use my change-at-the-fringes strategy. For example, I took my first acting class three years before I left corporate to try it professionally.

My first step was not to equate acting with leaving my job because that was too big a bite to swallow at the time. Ultimately I did leave my job, and it was the right step in order to fully attend auditions, immerse myself in classes, and have the time to try the many different things I needed to know the business well enough to progress. But initially I made a small change and kept everything else constant.

Keeping most things constant is a key part of my coaching approach with clients. One of the other first things I do with clients, aside from running the numbers, is take a 40-question assessment of where their life stands in a variety of different areas. Clients come to me for career-related goals, but I ask about finances, relationships, and self-care/personal issues. Why? Our lives are just one part career. If there is too much going on everywhere else, we may not have the bandwidth to add career moves. Better to get the rest in order and come back to the career issues. Or drop the other projects altogether and focus just on career for a little while to get traction.

Many people don't like their jobs. This doesn't have to mean running away and joining the circus. The first change at the fringe might be to keep doing your job but change what you do one night a week – you take a class in your new field, you join an industry group in your new field, you reserve the night to reach out to your network. Then you add more fringe changes on other nights and perhaps weekends before you change beyond the fringes.

When trouble arises and things look bad, there is always one individual who perceives a solution and is willing to take command. Very often, that individual is crazy – Dave Barry

Ultimately, though, to effect a big career change you have to do the crazy thing and leave your job to join the circus (or in my case be an actor which is really the same thing). Changing at the fringes only works for so long because at some point you will have changed all the fringes and your only moves left are big ones. But since fringe changes are subtle, most people around you won't notice. Then when you do make the big move, it looks abrupt, fanciful, irresponsible and crazy.

You want to start a business in the middle of a recession? Of course you can!

You want to change careers from accounting to music? The best time is now!

You want to ask for a raise and promotion while your industry descends into flames? Let's ask for even more.

These are all real-life examples of clients who made big moves that could easily be perceived by others as crazy. My advice was more extensive than the pithy shorthand above, but essentially I gave those recommendations. I encouraged my clients to make these "crazy" moves because they already did the small stuff to support the move, and they still wanted more. You can only get more when you do more. You can only get something different when you do things differently. The real craziness is to do the same things and expect something else to happen. If you don't like your job, you will have to change how you feel or the job itself, but you will have to change something.

Courage is not the absence of fear but rather the judgment that something else is more important than fear – Ambrose Redmoon

Eventually, I wasn't afraid anymore that leaving my corporate life to try acting was the sure path to homelessness. I ran the numbers and realized I could save and freelance my way to the financial safety net that worked for me. I made small moves before the crazy one to build my confidence and work out any kinks in my initial plans. And finally, I decided there was something more important than the fear of failing at acting....

Instead of fearing acting, I decided to fear regret! Look, I am a fearful person. I was not able to happy talk myself into dismissing something so core to my DNA. But as I peeled back the layers of my fear (and it was baklava, millefoglia, Spanish onion-sized) I realized that my biggest fear wasn't the money I would lose. I could get that back. It wasn't the corporate stature. I could also get that back.

What I couldn't get back was the time, and therefore I used the "what if" fear. If I didn't do this now and something happened that meant I never did, could I live with not doing it? No, I couldn't live with that, and that scared me even more. Thus it was this bigger fear that quenched my other fears and encouraged me to go for it.

I do believe in thinking abundantly and positively. But I also believe in harnessing fear. When you're as fearful as I am, it is a natural resource to take advantage of. More importantly, sometimes the best way to fight fear is with fear. Sometimes the biggest changes happen when you're scared into change: the employee from a shrinking industry that finally makes a move because layoffs loom; the closet entrepreneur who finally takes a risk when a loved one dies and they see firsthand that later might not come; the unhealthy person who makes radical life changes after a medical scare.

The money we receive in return for our eight hours of work each day can be spent any number of ways; the only thing we cannot buy is extra time. So, during the minutes we have, I believe it is better to live a dream rather than to simply dream it. The dream is the start of something greater, something that impels us to make daring decisions. And it's true that the person who pursues a dream takes many risks. But the person who does not runs risks that are even greater. -- Paulo Coelho

Fear can be very motivating when you harness it to make the changes you want to make. Remind yourself that time is not renewable and moves unnoticed. How often do we say, "Where did the time go?" Remind yourself how bad it feels to realize that time has gone and you still haven't done what you always wanted to do. When you feel yourself fearing failure or bankruptcy or disapproval, remember that most things we fear losing can be regained or reclaimed. But we can never get back the time we lose that could have been spent on our dreams. Do you really want to risk having to ask yourself what might have been? If you think change is scary, try regret.

*   *   *   *   *   *   *

Caroline Ceniza-Levine is a career coach, writer, speaker, Gen Y expert, life coach (www.thinkasinc.com), and co-founder of SixFigureStart (www.SixFigureStart.com), a career coaching firm comprised of former Fortune 500 recruiters. Caroline teaches Professional Development at Columbia University and writes advice columns for CNBC.com Executive Careers and Vault.com Insider Career Advice. She has over 15 years of professional services experience in strategy consulting, retained search and corporate HR, including recruiting for Accenture, Booz Allen & Hamilton, Citibank, Disney ABC, Pfizer, TV Guide and Time Inc. Prior to her corporate career, Caroline was a classical pianist with a Diploma from the Juilliard School of Music and currently stays active in the arts, performing improv. A native New Yorker, she lives in Manhattan with her husband and two daughters.

Visit http://tinyurl.com/sfs-gym-pass to get a free pass to the SixFigureStart small group coaching "Coaching Gym" and experience firsthand how you can get the support you need to finally move past your fear and towards your dream.

Setting Fear Aside
Valarie Davenport Willis

We all fear something. I say we have to set fear aside, put it in its place. But you cannot set fear aside, like you can place a book on a shelf. A book is tangible-- you can see it, touch it, pick it up and put it away in its proper place. Fear has its place, but it is a temporary one.

Fear is invisible--you can't touch it or pick it up. But you can sense it in yourself and in others. Fear seems to ooze out of the pores of a body like the fragrance of a heavy perfume. We know when others are living in fear as their actions and behaviors seem to be erratic and irrational.

What if we could learn to turn the energy of fear into our dreams? That is what I try to do when I am facing fear. I channel my energy into my dreams and my goals.

I grew up in a household where I never saw fear from my parents. I am sure that there were times when they felt fear, but as a child, I never saw it. We were taught to stand up for ourselves, to do the best that we could and frankly, failure was not an option in our house. Because of that, I have always tried very hard to push fear aside or to push it deep down into some internal cavern of my body in hopes that it will stay hidden and tucked away. I often don't claim the existence of my fears. Rarely will you hear me admit to fear, but the reality is, I have fear, I just don't articulate it out loud. I have learned to set fear aside and move forward.

But burying fear does not make it go away. To control fear, I learned that I must first own it, confront it and admit that I am fearful. I experience fear just like anyone else and there are so many situations and challenges in my life that can bring fear out. I know when fear is around— it seems to engulf me like flames from a fire. Fear is like paralysis, my brain can't function, I can't breathe right, and I feel totally disoriented.

Fear changes my entire persona; it is as if I become another person, the way the Incredible Hulk transforms into someone new. However, even the Hulk returns to normal when he gets the situation under control. That is the way I view fear; I try to get it under control, before it controls the very essence of my being and turns me into an unrecognizable person.

A few years ago, I worked for an organization that had faced some serious sales issues. We had re-structured the company, took pay cuts and made many other sacrifices. The business seemed to be improving. You can imagine how I felt when I was told that my job was being eliminated. After all the work, the changes, the sacrifices, and the long hours, it all seemed so unfair. I was being downsized!

The dreaded "D" word had reared its ugly face in my life. So, as much as I didn't want to claim fear, it claimed me!

The news of the downsizing threw me into a vortex of immobility. I couldn't catch my breath, my hands were clammy and I was perspiring profusely. I thought I was sick, that it must be the flu. It was. It was the "fear flu."

I just couldn't think clearly or function well. I found myself replaying the downsizing conversation in my head over and over, like a broken record. I was stuck in the moment and I was paralyzed. I kept focusing my attention on the downsizing and what impact it would have on me, my family, and others who depended on me.

Looking back, my attention and focus had been on the wrong matter. I was living in the past and not moving forward. The more I focused on the past, the more fear could penetrate the walls of sanity, and the more irrationally I would think.

Have you ever allowed your attention to be so focused on the past that you can't see your way clear to the future? Our fearful thoughts are like a veil we hide behind that obscures our view of the future. That veil separates us from the opportunities that await us. We need to push the veil away so that we can have a clearer view of our possibilities.

To push the veil away, we have to clear our heads. To do this effectively I go on walks. Some days it can be hard to even think about moving forward or going for a walk. So, I trick my mind, even when I hear the brain saying, "No, don't move, stay here. Fear will keep you company."

The key is to set a destination. Sometimes the destination is just to go to the park, or it may be a certain number of streets I will walk before I turn around. The goal is to get out and go, so your brain can refresh itself. It's similar to hitting the reset key on the computer; you get to "reboot" the brain.

Friends can also be one of the best antidotes for fear. After the downsizing, one of my girlfriends who recognized my symptoms of fear, called me every morning, bright and early for a week. She would ask me what I had done, who I had spoken to, and what I was going to do that day. Being accountable to someone put a new spin on the picture. It started moving me forward.

The breakthrough moment came when we were talking about a speech she had recently done and she said to me, "You could develop a speech or book, have you thought about that?"

I am not sure what intrigued me about her remarks, but immediately I could see the book in my head. It was enough to move me into action and set fear aside. We have to find the triggers that will help us move past fear. The book idea was my trigger. I immediately wrote the concept down, came up with a title and every day, I would look at the title to remind me to keep moving on it. Having a visual image of where you want to be can boost your spirits enough to keep you going.

The book project gave me purpose and passion. Finding that magical combination of purpose and passion can help you break through fear. All of a sudden you have something new to occupy the space that fear invaded, you have something to get energized about and you can start to see a glimpse of the future. The veil is being lifted.

My book was entitled, *Words for Women from A-Z*. It is about how we need to choose our words carefully, and which words we should have in our vocabulary to keep us going when times get tough. The words we speak lift us up or deflate us. You can become a victim of your own words and of fear. We have choices and we have to learn to choose. I choose not to live in fear. I choose to channel my energies into my dreams. What do you choose to do?

Working on the book got me to the place where I could tell fear, "Not on my watch will you stay. You are not welcome here." Sometimes we have to speak those words out loud, so that they echo back into our brains. Tell fear to "Take a hike." Choose every day, not to let fear reside in you.

After finishing it, my book helped to open doors for speaking engagements and book sales. I became a national keynote speaker for a major organization and I know that would never have happened, if I hadn't turned fear into dreams.

After the downsizing, I started my own consulting firm. The current economic tsunami has hit my business and others pretty hard, but doing nothing or being fearful is not the answer.

My father has a motto from Charles Swindoll that says, "I am convinced that life is 10% what happens to me and 90% how I react to it." That motto has served me well. A change in our attitude is like making a mental shift. Just as you shift a car to change gears, depending on driving conditions, you can shift your mental attitude into a higher gear. You have a choice-- choose to let go of fear. I find that when I approach a situation with a positive attitude and can see a positive outcome, life is a lot more fun!   I tell people I have been outsized, right-sized, downsized and transitionized, but I have survived! And so shall you.

Set fear aside by:

Choosing not to live with fear. Tell yourself, "No fear today."

Clear your head through some form of exercise.

Find a project that you can be passionate about and allow your energy to focus on that project and not on the fear.

Put your attitude into high gear through writing or journaling.

Keep moving forward, one step at a time.

Stay connected to positive friends. Set goals with them for accountability.

Have the courage to keep moving forward and stay positive. Lastly believe in yourself, your abilities and your talents. Remember that each of us has a purpose in life and we live to fulfill that purpose and our dreams. Setting fear aside will allow us to achieve more than we can possibly imagine.

*　　*　　*　　*　　*　　*

Valarie Davenport Willis is an accomplished speaker, facilitator, consultant, trainer and executive coach, focused in the area of leadership, branding, innovation and change.

Known for her passion and energy, Valarie has worked with companies in many industries including health care, pharmaceutical, government, manufacturing, wholesale, retail, technology and finance. Her mission is to guide and provoke organizations to optimize business results through leadership development and brand experiences.

She is author of *Words for Women* and is featured in the leadership anthology, *Leading the Way to Success*. Valarie is also a contributing writer for business publications, such as "Leadership Excellence" and Sales & Marketing Excellence. You may contact her through Valarie Willis Consulting: www.valariewillisconsulting.com; val@valariewillisconsulting.com 513-677-5637.

The Price of Fear
Cherry-Ann Carew

While on holiday in London, I bumped into an acquaintance - I'll call her Sheila, who is a friend of my former neighbor—Christine, not her real name—whom I had not seen for years before I immigrated to the United States from England. She was all smiles as she approached me with outstretched arms.

"Oh my God! I was asking Christine for you the other day. For some reason I had a mental block and couldn't remember your name. I said, you know, the rich one with the fancy house and flash car..." she gushed in, I am sure, one breath.

If my hands were not laden with shopping, I would have gasped and covered my mouth. She could not have been referring to me. I looked around in confusion, as I certainly did not fit the description she portrayed.

Rich was in my life, yes. I had two, young, beautiful children, family, friends, acquaintances and even a cat, all who loved me – my life was abundant with the richness of love. But the rich that Sheila made inference to seemed to be of the monetary kind and it was not yet in my life back then.

Those years <u>back then</u>, exploded into my consciousness. Yes, by definition, I owned a house that I was hanging onto by barely paying the interest that was a hefty liability – fancy! I guess that is open to interpretation. Flash car! It was a second-hand Ford Escort GTI for God sakes, with a dent at the front side that I could not afford to fix, and it wasn't even a soft top.

In addition, there were the usual shopping, utility and credit card bills I was juggling to pay.

Furthermore, I had recently severed a long-term relationship. In the blink of an eye, I was left to run a household—that started with two salaries—on a school grant as I was at university. I also became a single parent. Not long after, I, thankfully, graduated.

At that time, rich was a distant dream and financial fear was my enemy.

I never did like being held hostage by 9 to 5 jobs, so armed with my degree I felt I could conquer the world. Instead of rejoining corporate England, I sought freelance work as a writer and researcher. I do believe I spent more time running after clients for payment; lack of money was a constant as I continued to juggle.

One day, I went to collect a check for a research job I did for a client. He had been fobbing me off for months and as I was down to... well, zero pounds, only to be told that he was out of the country and would not return for another two weeks.

I stood staring down the barrel of reality for a while then remembered walking back to my car with a sinking feeling thinking, *I have no money in my bank account. My credit cards are exhausted. I don't even have enough for my kid's school dinner and I have no one to turn to.* Everyone I knew was struggling financially too.

It is noteworthy to say here, that I ran as I heaved from a fear that rose from the pit of my stomach and before I knew it, exercised projectile vomiting. I was clearly unpracticed, as I didn't get anywhere close to the receptacle I aimed for.

It took me over an hour to get home because of the rush hour traffic. I peered at the slowly changing traffic lights through clouds of condensing exhausts, and the intermittent swish-swish of wipers.

The house that was my home was dimly lit and the passage light was on. The weather was cold. The scattered yellow and reddish-brown, slippery mulch of fallen leaves that littered the pavement and the entrance to my door was not an unusual sight. It was the middle of the autumn season.

I paused and looked at the house. I had fallen in love with its Tudor style features the first time I saw it. For a moment, I felt like a stranger standing before the concrete structure. I may well have to sell it, I thought, except, if it couldn't be sold, where would my children and I go?

I took a deep breath and opened the door. The softly lit warmth of the interior walls was a welcome contrast to the darkness I felt inside my being. I went to my room, grateful for the solitude. I needed time to comprehend the situation I was in and most importantly, find a way out of my financial rut.

That night, I couldn't sleep, for in my abstraction of day-to-day living, I had not looked beyond my wages to save for a rainy day and it was downright pouring at that moment.

I wrote a list of my debts. I then drew a circle and used arrows to note sources that I could contact to borrow some funds, including the bank; I already had a loan with them. The chart looked like spiders with elongated tentacles. After mulling over it for a while, I realized that no financial institution would give me a loan without proof of fulltime employment.

I wanted to heave again; instead, I drew a line from one end of the paper to the other and wrote, 'never again'. I made a pact with myself that night that I was never going to be in a position where I did not have money-- ever again.

A few months later, I was in the United States on a 3-month contract working as a recruiter, a role that was new to me and held little interest. It was the longest time I would be away from my home and my children. The money was rubbish, and so too was my bipolar boss, but I wasn't getting anywhere with freelance work on my home turf. I had to look for new opportunities.

Career wise, my priority was to become a fulltime fiction writer. The problem was that it would not bring in a fixed income.

I returned to London after my recruiting stint and over the following years, I took anything that would put food in my children's mouths. I freelanced in the writing arena and commenced writing a novel that I put on ice every so often due to work and family commitments.

Out-of-the blue, the publisher for a sports journal offered me the position of editor. Shortly after, I got the opportunity to move to the U.S. and decided to go. Some of my friends and family were thrilled for me; others couldn't believe I was giving up a good job and my home to go to a foreign country without any support mechanism.

I had to do it. A good job wasn't enough. I had bigger plans and I didn't feel they would materialize in England. So I sold my home and used some of the equity to pay off my debts then immigrated to California, where I continued to work as an editor. Within two months of my arrival, the publication folded owing me thousands of pounds in wages.

Deja vu - I didn't heave this time. I was winded. I felt as if a boxer had jabbed me in my solar plexus. There I was, an alien, in an alien country without a job and little money. I had to roll with the punches, to coin an overused cliché. I placated myself that my once-again-unemployment status was simply an intermission.

I defrosted my manuscript and indulged in a literary workout while I sought employment. I devoured any book I could find relative to writing, went to creative workshops and took any free courses on and off line.

I was ahead of the game in comparison to many novice writers whom I encountered and soon I was asked to copyedit people's manuscripts. Before I knew it, I was also coaching on the mechanics of writing. I thoroughly enjoyed helping people in our shared passion--and they paid me. I could turn this into a business I thought.

By happen stance, I was invited to go into a joint-partnership in the recruiting field with a friend—he liked my savvy go-getter attitude, he told me. First, I didn't enjoy my recruiting experience years back and second, I had no money to invest in a business venture.

However, I was in the land of opportunity and an opportunity presented itself. I did some research and found that recruiting was actually big business. I knew my strengths and talents. I knew if I put my mind to it, I could make a financial success of the company. I knew I could build it to the point whereby I could afford to put it in the hands of someone else that would allow me to follow my calling—writing.

My friend-turn-business partner agreed to finance the project and my investment was sweat! I would start up the company from the bottom up with the shares split sixty/forty.

I signed on the dotted line and enjoyed my new position initially because I wrote all the copy for the web site and the marketing materials. Within a year, I grew bored. I wasn't 'feeling' being a co-owner even with a grand title of executive director. But, I was on a consistent salary, versus sporadic editing and coaching after a long spate of being officially unemployed and penny pinching.

After much deliberation, I realized that I was being unfair to my business partner, who was a great person, by not giving the business my all.

Furthermore, I was being unfair to me. I was hindering my personal wants and desires by sabotaging my writing career, so I relinquished my partnership.

I did the unthinkable and took the biggest financial risk of my life. I borrowed thousands of dollars on a line of credit to start my own editing and coaching business.

It took a couple of years, in fact, a few, to ramp up; but my life has since crested. I completed my novel that is due for publication in 2010, wrote a series of e-books, and I am co-author of this anthology with some of the best of the best entrepreneurs.

Have I reached the zenith of my financial achievements? No, but with this new regeneration, my finances are more streamlined than when I last saw Sheila.

At this point, my attention returned to her squeals as she enveloped me in her arms

"Oh, hi," I managed, though I couldn't return the hug. "Sheila, right," I said and imploded with laughter.

My, I thought, how had the trajectory of my life curved since we last met?

* * * * * * *

Cherry-Ann Carew is a gifted independent writer, writing coach and copyeditor with over fifteen years experience in professional writing for various magazines, newspaper publications and online content.

She is the author of a novel that will be published by INDI Publishers later this year. She has also written a series of E-books under the umbrella title: In Layman Terms - *A Guide for Aspiring Writers* and is currently collaborating on a non-fiction book, entitled "Cook Up."

Cherry-Ann specializes in assisting novice writers to prepare their books for traditional and self-publication.

How to Handle Fear…
In Daily Life

The Day Fear Lied
Janet Slack

The sun wasn't even up yet that hot Florida morning as my husband and I jogged slowly down the street. I was doing my best to wake both my mind and my body. Suddenly, I realized he was no longer beside me and I turned to see what had slowed him down. He was sprawled across the ground in the midst of a fatal heart attack. I was 32 years old and my world exploded into chaos. My life would never be the same.

The following days, months, years were filled with the processes of grief. Interwoven with the grief was always fear. My heart would be racing and I would be filled with dread or panic. Life hurt indescribably. Somewhere during the process, I noticed myself changing and becoming fierce. This is that story.

At first I didn't recognize the fear among so many other feelings. Within a week I was sitting in a lawyer's office hearing bad financial news. I had to return to work immediately or risk foreclosure on our house. In my fright, I could only imagine homelessness. At work, my mind was like quicksand; when asked questions, I panicked that I wasn't making sense. I spent a great deal of time in a ladies room stall shaking and tearful. Things were impossibly hard and I was scared that

I couldn't go on. I'd go into the grocery store and couldn't remember what I was there for. Then I had no idea what I should eat or how to buy for just one person. One day, with a bagger following me with my cart, I spent 15 minutes holding back tears of alarm while looking for my car in the parking lot.

I trudged through the first months trying to hold myself together. I lived in fear of falling apart. It was spring in Florida so the grass needed mowing every few days. I had never done it. After many days I braved myself to try it, doing everything I could imagine to make the lawnmower start. I ended up sobbing on the garage floor with the grass uncut. How many more things was I not going to be able to handle? How could I get through life if I couldn't even mow a lawn?

My husband and I had been living a thousand miles from where I was raised. Within a few months of his death, I began thinking of moving home even though you are not supposed to make major life decisions right after a tragic loss. Everyone had an opinion on what I should do, but I waffled for months over the decision. I was frightened to stay where life was so out of control, but afraid to make a mistake by moving. Perhaps if I were back where I had always been safe, I could find some other way to survive. Finally, I knew I had to go. My brother helped me and the move occurred despite shuddering apprehension.

Fear was always present in my mind, but I didn't necessarily know it and didn't identify all that made me afraid. I allowed no risks in my life. I lived in a house I had lived in before, worked for a former employer and spent time with a few old friends and my family. I stepped through each day staying with the safety of the familiar-- even the thought of something new caused my pulse to race. Fear had me penned in.

About 18 months after my husband's death, I was forced to deal with something new. A routine medical exam and lab results showed an abnormal Pap smear. The doctor said we couldn't just watch it, those dangerous cells had to be cut out.

Suddenly, the world was crashing in on me again. The one thing I could count on through all the hard times was my health. Although things might go wrong and life might be terribly frightening, I could count on my own body. Now the enemy, unpredictable and dangerous, was inside me. I told no one.

My mind did funny things as terror settled in. When I lay in bed, I saw myself having chemotherapy and saying goodbye to my family. I'd tell myself, "Don't be silly" and tried to picture myself running on the beach in ten years. Then before I knew it, I was imagining my own funeral. Was I really going to die alone? Finally I would force myself to remember the doctor's words, "This won't cause any big problems as long as we take care of it now."

It was difficult to force myself back to the doctor's office for the procedure. I was shivering and my mind was racing. I had a hard time sitting still as I waited for the surgery to begin. I barely noticed the doctor's attentiveness and that the procedure went well. When I rose to leave, I passed out instead. Fear had literally knocked me down.

I can still hear the soothing voice of the nurse, "It's all over. You are going to be just fine and there is nothing to worry about. You can just stay here for a while and rest." She massaged my head and shoulders while I calmed myself. I finally could hear and take into my heart that the crisis was over. I had survived and there were no expected long-term problems. Fear had lied.

My discovery that fear had lied was a turning point. My body had not betrayed me. When I looked back at my own reaction to a small medical issue, I knew fear had crept into my thoughts and had tried to take over. But most of all I could see that I had handled it in spite of run-away terror. I had walked through this event using something deep inside myself even while being attacked by fear.

I faced the two-year anniversary of my husband's death with dread. I needed to be alone and near the ocean, which always helped to heal my soul. I went to Cape Cod and walked the deserted March beaches. On the second day, I carried a box of tissues with me and wore my warmest coat. I sat on a dune, watched the ocean and cried over all that had occurred and all that might yet occur. After the tears, I was able to think.

Fear is an intriguing beast. After I caught it lying, it had taken a transformation that became my final hurdle in learning to be fierce. Fear was no longer about being alone, fear had become about being able to love again. Sitting on the dune alone, I thought about a very long life of loneliness ahead. Although I was terrified of going through so much pain again, I made a conscious choice to battle against fear. I chose not to be a bitter, lonely old woman.

I looked fear in the face. "Hell no, you're not going to win. I am a fighter. Didn't I bruise my own lips doing CPR? You're not going to get me that easily. There's more I can do." And I could feel fierce growing within me.

Over the previous two years, I had learned how to be okay alone. I had dated, but each man was someone who was obviously not a good choice for me. I went home from the Cape and broke up with the last one. Later I called a man I had known in high school and with whom I had recently exchanged a few letters. I was willing to get to know him more in spite of the fear. I knew I would be okay if he wasn't "the one" and I might be okay if he was. In a matter of months I realized that love was worth the risk and it didn't take us too many more months to decide to get married. Fierce worked.

When I agreed to be a part of this book and write about this time in my life, I was apprehensive. The apprehension turned to fear as the time for writing grew near. The death of my husband was the most painful thing that had ever happened to me. What was I thinking to let myself revisit that pain? How much would I need to relive in order to write what needed to be said? I talked to my current husband about the project. I collected ideas from others on how best to take care of myself and I stepped carefully into the process. As I write, I realize I have great power in being able to revisit this and stay in control. The inevitable return of fear is another opportunity to defeat it. My fierceness muscle grows with use.

I no longer give fear the space in my life it had before. I no longer feed it and help it to grow. Now when fear walks in, I ask for help, gain strength from others, and access that place within where fierceness resides. I remember all the times in daily life that I act in spite of being afraid. I need to face fear periodically to keep it in perspective - to stare it down and stay in my newly discovered power and freedom. Standing fierce in the face of fear opens new vistas in the adventure of my life.

On a recent trip to Alaska, I learned about grizzly bears and how to survive a grizzly attack. Our Alaskan guide announced to us carefully that a grizzly had just been seen in the area. He gave clear directions to stay together and not to run – no matter what. Grizzlies often charge a target to see what it will do. If it runs, it is prey. It is no surprise that nature tests our balance between fear and fierceness. It tests us and determines our survival based on the answer. In a grizzly bear charge, acting on fear creates danger, while acting with fierce courage creates safety. I know today, that I can stand up to the grizzly charge.

*　　*　　*　　*　　*　　*

Janet Slack is owner of Life Adventure Coaching (http://life
adventurecoaching.com) and Solopreneur.biz (http://solopreneur.biz).
Her first book, *Mind Your Own Biz*, is a guide to starting and developing
a coaching business. Her passion is coaching people to succeed in life
through seeking fun, challenges and rewards whether they are small
business owners, women in transition or even those conquering fear
and learning to find joy. Her background includes developing a thriving
coaching business, completing a master's degree in counseling, starting
a counseling private practice, studying for an MBA, and working as
a manager and consultant in the environmental field. She and her
husband live and play in the mountains of Western North Carolina.
Janet invites you to connect with her by email through her websites.

False Experiences
Appearing Real
Jordan McAuley

"Fear will keep you alive in war. Fear will keep you alive in business. There's nothing wrong with being afraid at all."
—Norman Schwarzkopf

My father loves to tell me about how his father taught him how to swim by throwing him out of a boat in the middle of the ocean. I'm not sure if it's true or not, but it probably was. He learned to swim that day, went on to fly helicopters in Vietnam after high school, picking up wounded soldiers in enemy territory, and won a Purple Heart for his heroic efforts. He of course experienced fear I could never imagine, but never gave up. He went on to become CEO of a large, very successful commercial real estate company, telling me one day that the reason he was able to survive in Vietnam was because of his positive mental attitude… that and never giving up.

One of my very first jobs in high school was working at a local video store. One night the owner of the sandwich shop next door came over to tell us that one of his employees had been robbed at gunpoint. Surely it was a one-time robbery that would not happen again, at least to us, we thought. We were wrong. The next night, we were the targets.

Fortunately I wasn't there, but that night the robber pointed a gun at my co-worker and told her to go in the back office, close the door and count to ten. I can't imagine the fear she must have endured. When she finally got the nerve to open the door and walk back into the store, the gunman had left and all of the money was gone. She quit that night.

A few days later, when two girls in my high school class were visiting a friend of mine who also worked with me at the store, they were robbed again, all three of them. Again I wasn't working that night, but asked my father if I should keep going back to work since our store had now been robbed twice at gunpoint. "You don't have a choice," he said. "Great!" I quickly thought. He wouldn't make me go back to work and I would have the rest of the year off until I graduated. Then he went on: "If you want me to pay for college, you're going back to work." I kept going back to work, after almost all the other employees quit, and was promptly promoted with a pay raise because I stayed. And that was the day I learned not to quit.

As young as I can remember, my father was always telling me to have a "positive mental attitude." That isn't something you want to hear when you're having problems in school… "Just have a positive mental attitude!" It drove me crazy. All of the personal success tapes and books in his library and in his car could suck it, I thought to myself. Today, after studying successful coaches such as Napoleon Hill, Jack Canfield, Dan Kennedy, and Lee Milteer for my business, I know that a positive mental attitude… and never giving up… is the secret to conquering fear.

One of my favorite quotes from Tony Robbins about the Law of Attraction that best sums up how to conquer fear for me is, "Whatever you dwell on grows in your experience. Ask yourself what you do want, not what you don't want."

One of my favorite "celebrity mentors" is Madonna. Talk about a fearless woman who went from nothing to not doing too shabby for herself! Looking at her now, people forget that she came from a working class family with a single father, moved to New York City with only $35 in her pocket, lived on the streets of Times Square, and pursued her dream until she became one of the most famous women in the world. Why? Because she never allowed fear to rule her life, much less enter her mind. And she never gave up. One of my favorite Madonna songs is on one of her very first albums called "Over and Over." The lyrics that she wrote in 1983 are:

Hurry up, I just can't wait
I gotta do it now I can't be late
I know I'm not afraid I gotta get out the door
If I don't do it now I won't get anymore
You try to criticize my drive
If I lose I don't feel paralyzed
It's not the game it's how you play
And if I fall I get up again now

I get up again, over and over
I get up again, over and over
I get up again, over and over
I get up again, over and over

Got past my first mistake
I'll only give as much as I can take
You're never gonna see me standin' still
I'm never gonna stop 'till I get my fill

It doesn't matter who you are
It's what you do that takes you far
And if at first you don't succeed
Here's some advice that you should heed

You get up again, over and over
You get up again, over and over
You get up again, over and over
You get up again, over and over

I try to remember these lyrics when things aren't going right. One of my friends, a very successful television host and interior designer, turned the lyrics into a painting and has it hanging on the wall of his home. These lyrics have inspired many people to conquer fear and "get up again, over and over."

When I was living in Los Angeles growing my business, I got a phone call from my father one night. "Are you sitting down?" he asked. "Your mother has colon cancer." Our whole family was scared, and I cannot imagine the fear my mother must have been going through. But we went on, kept a positive mental attitude, and never gave up. I'm proud to say she beat the cancer. Soon after, my brother announced he was joining the Army, and a year later was sent off to Iraq during the middle of the war, missing both Thanksgiving and Christmas at home. Again, my family was terrified, but he returned home safely, and is now a Commander. I cannot imagine the fears my family has experienced: My father being drafted to Vietnam; my mother being diagnosed with cancer; and my brother being shipped off to Iraq. When I think about those fears, nothing about running a business is scary. It helps put what we experience as entrepreneurs into perspective.

One of the biggest fears entrepreneurs face is the fear of public speaking. Experts say that more people are afraid of public speaking than they are of death. I'm not so sure that's true... if I had to choose to get up in front of a group and speak or be killed, I think I'd choose to speak in front of a group! But it is a very real fear. I try to remember what my father, mother, and brother had to go through when I'm asked to get up and speak. Would I rather speak than go into war? YES! Would I rather speak than have to go through cancer treatment? YES! When we put things into perspective, it really helps to conquer fear.

A natural introvert, I've never enjoyed public speaking. But as a business owner, it's something we have to do, especially if we want to grow both personally and professionally. What's helped me the most with this is doing it little by little over time. If you're afraid of public speaking, join a group like Toastmasters or take a Dale Carnegie class. What's so hard in the beginning is the rush of adrenalin that can either make us too animated or almost paralyzed, depending on how we react to stress. Doing little talks to a welcoming audience over time helps desensitize our bodies and our minds to this stress. So after a while, it gets easier and easier. As we build up to larger groups and practice giving larger talks, we realize there's nothing to be afraid of.

Positive psychology says FEAR really stands for "False Experiences Appearing Real." I first heard this from one of my mentors, Lee Milteer, author of *Success is an Inside Job*. It really is true. Fear is what you make it. There are bigger things to be afraid of in life than what we experience running a business. But even if we have to go through some of those bigger trials, it helps to have a positive mental attitude and never give up. Remember, what you focus on expands. Keep focusing on the positive and you'll conquer fear in no time!

*   *   *   *   *   *   *

CELEBRITY | PR (www.CelebrityPR.com) Founder **Jordan McAuley's** record spans more than a decade in publicity, marketing, publishing and events. Known as the "King of Celebrity Contacts," his Contact Any Celebrity (www.ContactAnyCelebrity.com) service is one of the most respected publicity resources in the world, with a blue-chip roster of over 5,000 marketers, publicists, nonprofits and media clients who rely on it to get endorsements, donations, interviews, and more.

He is the author of the best-selling annual directory, *The Celebrity Black Book*, *Secrets to Contacting Celebrities*, and *Celebrity Leverage: Insider Secrets to Getting Celebrity Endorsements, Instant Credibility and Star-Powered Publicity*.

You can visit ContactAnyCelebrity.com to search his online database containing constantly updated contact information for of over 60,000 celebrities and public figures worldwide.

How I Took Flight From Rock Bottom
Raychelle LeBlanc

I have always had a special relationship with fear. As a child I remember being chased around a parking lot by what I thought was a dog, only to find out that it was the zipper on the back of my dress that had me running for dear life. Had I known then what I know now, I would have been perfectly content running from zippers instead.

The Spiral

I am still not 100% sure when I decided to allow fear and anxiety to alter my life. I remember driving down the sunny California highway and being hit by what felt like a brick wall. I couldn't breathe, my palms were sweaty, my heart felt like it was beating out of my chest and I had the most incredible urge to flee and get off the freeway, immediately. That was my first introduction to a panic attack but it certainly would not be my last. I was determined to never experience that feeling again and that determination prevented me from driving on the freeway for the next 3 years. I had to get up extra early for work to drive the side streets, and if I was riding with someone I had to swallow the panic that welled up every time I was convinced that the freeway was "way faster than the side streets".

There are many other examples to share of how fear changed the course of my life. I didn't feel comfortable sharing what I was feeling because it felt "silly" and I was embarrassed to try and explain. It would have been even more difficult to explain while in the midst of an attack. How do you explain that you feel like you are getting ready to make the "big drop" on the mega rollercoaster while standing perfectly still? Or that you could have the incredible urge to run out of the room in the middle of a conversation? Not only did I assume that people would be offended, but they would also think that I was a crazy person. I had allowed this fear to transform me from an outgoing, friendly and lively person to a homebody out of fear of having a panic attack in public. My friends and family had no idea what was going on with me but they could definitely see that there was a change in my day- to- day habits.

The Pit

Because I was always anxious I wasn't eating. My stomach was always upset and I starting losing weight. Home felt like my only safe haven. I was no longer interested in going to hang out with the girls or going clubbing with the crew. The fear had gotten so bad that if I was not able to visualize myself at work, I was not able to go. Being borderline agoraphobic was not working for me. I felt like I was in a dark pit and the sides were getting higher and higher. Although the "fear dialogue" that I was having with myself was internal, it was wreaking havoc on my life. When the mere thought of getting out of the bed and facing the world became a struggle from day to day, I knew that I was in trouble and that something had to be done.

Light at the Top End of The Tunnel

One of the first things that I did was seek out as much information as I could about panic attacks and anxiety. I had no idea that 40 million adults, 18 and over are affected by Anxiety Disorders and 6 to 7 million of them experience panic attacks and anxiety attacks (www. anxietypanic.com).

Journaling proved to be invaluable because I was able to see trends in when my anxiety peaked. That was important because I was able to identify any triggers and stay clear of them.

The next step was to share what I was going through with family and close friends. The support made all of the difference in the world. Being able to freely communicate what I was feeling proved to be key in minimizing my levels of anxiety in any given situation. It also served as a distraction as again, much of my conversation around the fear was with myself; what if this, what if that? Having someone around to talk to created a distraction and the fear often times subsided.

I would say the most important part of the work for me was the work that I had to do alone. During my research I discovered all of the medication that was available for panic attacks and anxiety disorders, none of which was I interested in taking. I went to visit my doctor and received a clean bill of physical health, went to visit my priest and received a clean bill of religious health so I set out on a quest to nurture my spiritual health. This was when the shift starting happening.

While journaling I discovered that however I went to bed is how I woke up so I started a ritual of sorts. It included my favorite music, candles and a good book, often times the Bible, Susan Taylor's book *In The Spirit* or anything by Iyanla Vanzant. I immediately stopped watching the news at night, as I didn't want to fill my mind with any negative thoughts or images right before bedtime. And finally, the last thing that I did before closing my eyes for the night was to pray and meditate. The silence was calming and helped me to clear my mind and create positive thoughts and ideas as I drifted off to sleep. This was my routine for a whole year. I still fall into this when I find myself getting too hectic or overwhelmed with work, thoughts and ideas.

Meditating gave me clarity to see that I was not content with certain things in my life and that led to my 1- year plan. When this plan was complete and in black and white I had to read it twice. I could not believe that it included a career change and a date to give my 2 weeks' notice. Trusting and surrendering had become a part of my new process so I went with it.

Taking Flight

I left my job in November of 1997 and was in New York by March of 1998. I could not believe that I was 3000 miles away from home 2 years after I was not able to leave my house without having heart palpitations. This process was grueling for me but fear was no longer an option. I am happy to report that I have been in New York for 11 years and have not looked back. Although I still experience fear, it is not unrealistic and I can acknowledge it and move through it. It is no longer allowed to rule my thoughts and actions.

Looking back on this dark part of my journey, there are 5 key things that were instrumental in overcoming my fear:

1) Communicate – The decision to discuss what I was experiencing with my support system was key! Allow your family

and friends to be there for you. Mine were extremely supportive and served as buffers when I felt like my fear was bigger than myself. Don't be afraid to seek professional help.

2) Breathe – Often times in the middle of a panic attack I realized that I was not breathing. Taking several deep, long breaths through my nose and exhaling though my mouth helped me to refocus and stay on task. I still do this when I am feeling overwhelmed.

3) Stay present – When you feel yourself getting worked up about a scenario that will most likely never happen, look around. Absorb your environment and take stock in what it is you are intending to do RIGHT now.

4) Acknowledge your fear – This will diminish the power that the fear will have over you. Realize that how you are feeling while in the middle of your anxiety or panic attack is ok. Just don't allow it to prevent you from doing what you set out to do. Feel it come and go and do it anyway!

5) Surrender – As a Christian woman this was the hardest part for me because I didn't understand how I got to this place in the first place. My journaling, reading and meditating showed me that I was not trusting in the process of our Creator. Accepting that fact that I was not in control and that there was a great force at work allowed me to relax and let go.....to trust and surrender.

*　　*　　*　　*　　*　　*

Raychelle LeBlanc started a career in entertainment in 1995 in the city of San Diego, California. She launched SheNotes Entertainment in 1999, a small boutique company specializing in Communications, Marketing and Special Events. Being a strong networker and seeing a need for connectedness among industry professionals, Raychelle graciously accepted numerous invitations to speak on panels and at workshops about networking and how to transition from where you are to where you want to be. Currently she is developing a series of workshops titled "Cake Everyday" that focus on celebrating life daily. Raychelle can be reached at shenotes@gmail.com.

How to Handle Fear…
With Spirituality

Get Off Your Knees
and Start Walking
Frank McKinney

A group of guys and I were on the team plane for the Orlando Magic, a 737 flying from West Palm Beach to Orlando. No, I wasn't hanging out with the players; I was traveling with Rich DeVos and his buddies, most of whom were in their late seventies to early eighties, some of whom he'd known since kindergarten. (It's just one of the many things I admire about Rich: how he keeps friends over decades.) Despite the fact that they were all significantly older than I was, balding, and wearing suits or business casual attire while I was in my usual rocker-meets-real-estate clothes, I felt completely at home. Rich has that effect on people.

Still, not long after we took off, one of the guys leaned in, tilted his head in my direction, and asked Rich, "Who's *that?*" Like most people do when they are hard of hearing, he was shouting although he thought he was being more discreet. Since no one but me could hear very well, I was the only one who noticed. So I pretended I didn't hear him and allowed the two old friends to continue their conversation uninterrupted.

"Oh, that's Frank McKinney," Rich told him, and then explained to the gent what I do for a living, emphasizing my renown for taking incredible risks in creating the most beautiful mansions in the world on spec. "Don't pay attention to his clothes or his long hair," he cautioned, waving his friend closer. Then he half-whispered, "That's just part of his *commercial.*"

The man nodded seriously, as if Rich had solved some deep riddle. I covered my laughter and thought, *how like Rich, to cut right through the surface level and get to the heart of things!* I appreciate what he said: If you strip away what Rich calls my "commercial"—my appearance and even my product (the mansions)—what really sets me apart, especially in business, is my ability to embrace risk in the face of fear. If there's anything I have claimed absolute mastery over on many occasions, it's risk. That doesn't mean I've made fear go away, or that I'm willing to risk everything for anything. It means that I understand risk at a level few people do and have learned to live with fear *every day*.

My ability to do this has been built over a long period of time; professionally, I wasn't born this way. For six years, I bought and sold first-time homebuyer foreclosure houses before I ever moved to high-end properties on the oceanfront. The first broken-down house I bought and fixed up sold for $50,000. The next jump was paying $50,000 for five burnt-out and boarded up buildings that eventually became known as the Historic Executive Suites of Delray—after I renovated them with $250,000, which was more than I'd ever invested at one time in one project. The first time I bought an oceanfront property, I took on an even greater level of risk, and each successive purchase after that has ratcheted up the risk yet again. My ability to handle the pressures I do now was built on that first purchase, and I don't pretend in any way that I could successfully risk what I do today if I hadn't experienced and learned from what could be perceived as much less risky deals in the past. Which one do you imagine inspired greater fear for me: my first $36,000 investment in a foreclosure house, or the tens of millions I put into an oceanfront creation today? I can assure you that first one was the hardest.

Likewise, my responses to Tap Moments have increased incrementally. As you know, I started out delivering meals from the back of a van. (Incidentally, that old Ford Econoline was so beat up and rusty that the spare tire would fall out of the bottom between stops!) My early, modest contributions laid the foundation for what we do today, and there were many steps in between: installing a mailbox for a physically handicapped man, painting a fence for a homebound woman, helping someone install new windows in place of broken ones, renovating little houses domestically and then leasing them for one dollar a month to elderly people who were homeless, taking our efforts overseas, and eventually building entire self-sufficient villages. Who knows what's next?

Risk tolerance and tap responsiveness are brother and sister, born out of opportunity and raised by consistent, conscious care.

In many ways, this chapter revolves around the central idea that you can tame your hesitation, uncertainty, lack of confidence, doubt, indecision, anxiety, or any other feeling of *fear* that's dressed up in another name. You can take action in spite of all that. You can do this by flexing your tolerance for risk like a muscle. You don't have to put millions on the line in your next business deal. You don't need to perform daredevil stunts or go 135 miles on foot in a race across the Death Valley desert and mountains. You don't have to provide housing for thousands of people. You don't have to do any of the dozens of things I do that may seem extreme to you. But you do have to learn to say yes, start, and overcome certain self-made obstacles that will get in your way. You *must* do this if you want to feel The Tap.

One of the most effective tools I offer to those people who seek my advice is a personal assessment of risk tolerance on a continuum from "phobic" to "daredevil." It was the foundation of one of the most popular chapters in my first book, *Make It BIG!* In that chapter, called "Gently Yet Often Exercise Your Risk Threshold Like a Muscle," you're invited to determine where you fall on the risk threshold continuum.

Risk Threshold Continuum
Phobic ----------------------------- Daredevil

If you're closer to phobic than daredevil, I say it's time to get into the risk threshold gym. Start building the muscle. Do something small for starters, then slowly increase the weight by seeking out larger opportunities with greater risk when you're ready. Keep pushing beyond your current comfort level, setting new standards for yourself, exceeding them, and then setting new ones again. This should take some time, and it should not be approached with blind haste.

Think about an area where you can do this right now: Have you been holding yourself back from accepting an invitation to speak in front of a group? Have you demurred from taking on more responsibilities at work? Have you been reluctant to join a movement you believe in? Have you still not acted on my encouragement to find a place where you can serve for even one day?

You can change all that with one decision and then act to close the loop. Notice I said one proactive act. That's all I want you to think about right now: just the one.

Decreasing your tap resistance is so similar to increasing your risk tolerance that I'm tempted to redirect you to Chapter 25 of *Make It BIG!*, because it made many of the points I'd stress to you here, and it did so exceptionally well. Risk tolerance and the risk continuum definitely have particular significance in the arena of The Tap. Certain principles especially apply:

To succeed in life, you must take risks. Those who enjoy success at higher levels tend to risk more than others—and resist The Tap less.

I'm scared all the time; I've just gotten used to it. Scared means something different to me: **a sensation resulting from the pursuit of an opportunity.**

How do you overcome the fear that accompanies risk? It's simple: **Start small.**

Deciding which risks to take is always a question of research and instinct. **Do your homework** to make sure the upside potential of the risk is good enough to make the effort worthwhile.

Opportunities always present fear and the choice to either take the risk or not. Because the only way to reap reward is by saying yes, while no can only lead to stagnation, **the greatest risk may be in not taking one at all.**

In the context of The Tap, we can think about risk in two ways: 1) acceptance of the belief that God rewards those who are responsible stewards of their blessings and that those blessings are to be shared even when you seem most vulnerable, even with no reward in sight, and 2) what's necessary for you to do in overcoming whatever resistance you may feel to acting on The Tap.

Moments of Perceived Silence

Sometimes it seems as if God isn't paying attention to you. When you have put yourself out there and begged for help with some endeavor, when you are at your most desperate and feel as if you're alone in this world without any spiritual support for you needs and desires, you may very well start asking God, "Is anybody listening?"

God could ask the same thing of you. **It's in those moments of deafening solitude, when it seems as if there's no answer to prayers, that you need to be most attentive and proactive, not shut down and self-centered.** At this time, when fear can reach its zenith, you must stay open to your upcoming Tap Moment, be waiting and watchful for an opportunity to do something for someone else.

This may sound counterintuitive, and I can assure you that the first few times you consciously choose to set aside your fear and instead be on alert for a Tap Moment, it can seem strange. But it's also liberating. You refocus. You stop dwelling on the thing that's not happening for you. You continue to act on your initiative, doing everything you know is necessary to achieve the objective, but you adjust your mindset, scanning the horizon for places to be of service, instead of worrying about whether or not you're going to get whatever it is you desire. I think of this as hearing *through* the perceived silence, instead of mistaking it for no answer (or a "no" answer).

One of the Caring House Project Foundation's champions provides us with an incredible example. I've known Doug Doebler since the early 1990s and watched his career take a meteoric rise and then seem to plummet back to earth. Through it all, he's held steadfast to his commitment to the people of Haiti—he has a lifetime of coincidences (some would call them "God-incidences") that make him believe that country is his Tap Moment vortex. It all started when he was a boy, and his aunt and uncle's church had raised funds to outfit a dental clinic in Port-au-Prince. His cousin had been hit by a car and killed when she was ten, and her parents placed a plaque over the door at the clinic to memorialize her. It was inscribed with his cousin's name and the phrase, *God is good.*

The first time I met Doug, I was delivering a keynote to a large business organization that, coincidentally, was focused on exercising one's risk threshold. Doug came up to me after my talk and mentioned that he had gone to Northwood University, a college where I sit on the Board of Governors and one of the least known but great colleges teaching the pursuit of free enterprise and capitalism in the United States. Although there were hundreds of people surrounding the autograph table, there was an aura about Doug that just seemed to cut through the crowd. We set a time the next day to meet in the lobby of the hotel to sit and talk. A few months after our initial meeting, in the spring of 2004, Doug wiped out his checking account to donate his last $20,000 to the Caring House Project Foundation, in exchange for an afternoon of personal success coaching, and we spent a twelve-hour day touring the mansions I had on the market at the time and enjoying an extended tree-house lunch together. Doug says that meeting prompted him to "think really big." Indeed, in the next two years, his business took off and he made millions, earning up to *sixty times* what he'd done in commissions in years past. He characterizes the 2005-2006 period as one of "extreme, unprecedented, and unexpected success." In 2007, he made another sizable donation to the foundation and accompanied our group to Cap-Haïtien in Haiti, where he flew over the very spot where he'd honeymooned nineteen years before (just one more of those many coincidences). After that trip, Doug was on fire, talking about Haiti with anyone who would listen, raising awareness about the conditions there, regularly and pointedly saying what a difference even a small contribution could make for the Haitian people.

Later that same year, the preconstruction condo market started to falter. The bubble seemed to burst. This meant that all of Doug's deals went south, buyers were losing big money, and Doug foresaw major lawsuits. Although he wasn't legally liable, that probably wouldn't keep some very angry and disappointed investors from trying to recoup their losses from him. In the ensuing months, he experienced a complete reversal of fortune. By January of 2008, Doug had gone a year with very little income, yet he felt so strongly about the impact he was making in Haiti that he borrowed $5,000 to make the donation required to build an entire home there, and then he traveled with us in February of that year. (During this time of nearly no income, by the way, Doug kept talking about Haiti, and I'm sure he influenced many donors to support our efforts there, although there's no way to know exactly how much money he caused to be sent our way. I do know of at least one businessman, Jim Whelan, who sat with Doug on an airplane, asked him for the name of our organization, and penned a $10,000 check on the spot. Jim is one of our largest benefactors today.)

When he returned home, Doug couldn't wait to once again share his experiences with anyone who would listen. In March, we were planning another trip for June, and he borrowed another $5,000, this time from himself, by spreading his donation over three credit cards so he could go with us, although his business bank accounts were, in his words, "pretty thin."

Just before we left for the June trip, Doug went to dinner with a developer he'd done business with in the past. In fact, the fellow had owed Doug $250,000 for more than a year, and Doug expected that debt would never be paid. In fact, he anticipated that they were going to ask Doug to return some of the commissions they had pad previously. The market was bad, and no one was honoring old debts. Yet, somewhere between the salad and the dessert—tap!—the developer handed Doug a check for the full amount. Where did that come from?!

Restate the Question

Who knows where the rest of Doug's story will go? Maybe he's at the beginning of another financial rise or, possibly, God has other plans for him. Tap Moments occur for reasons that are often beyond our comprehension, frequently contrary to our idea of what should or shouldn't happen in our lives, creating unexpected blessings.

Every now and then, they also present inconvenient twists and turns, redirecting our focus to something more important—at least for now. Whenever this is happening, you're wise to guard against interpreting it as a "no" or no answer at all. There've been many times when I have persisted in a certain direction, and it just hasn't turn out the way I'd hoped. Occasionally, it's seemed as if I've been abandoned in a kind of desert of the soul, yet *that's an illusion*. **The truth is that these periods are often vital gifts of time for reflection, providing a chance to revise the question, rethink the objective, restate the intention.**

Most recently, I've been completely gripped by the idea of designing, creating, then selling an estate worth a minimum of $135 million, inspired by Italian and Mediterranean architecture and planned for 67,672 square feet—The Manalapan Residence (http://www.frank-mckinney.com/estate_for_sale_manalapan_residence.aspx) would be an enormous place with a record-breaking price tag. In putting together a design and consultant team of more than twenty people, and getting the building permitted (four different permits from four governmental agencies, federal, state, county, and municipal—lots of red tape), I had to jump through major hoops, all of which took about a year. After that year, I had done it: designed and fully permitted the most beautiful megamansion in the world, complete with fourteen bedrooms, twenty-four bathrooms, an eighteen-car garage, a 6,140-square-foot master bedroom suite (three times the size of the average home), lavish Grand Rotunda room, dual water walls, aquarium ceilings and walls, movie theatre, casino and club room with stunning aquarium wet bar, his and her offices, ten wet bars, two wine rooms (one for red, one for white), gymnasium with beauty salon, two swimming pools (classical lap and grotto waterfall/waterslide), shark tank, two elevators, bowling alley, tennis court with pavilion, archery range, quarter-mile jogging/go-cart track, butterfly gardens, Italian and Floridian gardens, sculpture gardens, citrus orchard, guest house, staff house, and, well, I could go on and on...

After all that, when I went to the bank to close on the financing that I thought I had in place, the response was not at all what I'd expected: Given the current state of the market, we would like you to build and sell two smaller $30-40 million homes prior to the funding of this loan." *Wait a minute,* I was thinking. *I'm Frank McKinney, the real estate rock czar. My crystal ball is never wrong and all my projects turn to gold, so how can this be?* I was under the assumption that financing for this project was a done deal and had fully expected to get the money, based on my relationship with the bank and my impeccable credit history with them. But they said they wouldn't do it at this time.

Figuratively, I was standing there with the shovel in the ground—and when I was denied, it was as if they'd pulled the dirt right out from under me. I knew I could create this masterpiece, and I knew I could sell it, and as willing as I am to take big risks, I never do it foolishly. I knew I could make it happen, so I was completely convinced that the bank was denying me for no good reason. This was supposed to have been my crescendo. *Why was this occurring? God, I need your help! Hello? Are you listening?* It took me a cooling-off period and some deep reflection to finally come to accept that maybe it wasn't the right time to break ground on that particular project. In looking back, I think God was saying to me, "Slow down, young fellow. You're going a little too fast here. We're going to put the brakes on, and it isn't going to happen now."

At the time, I had to swallow my pride and agree to design and create two new estate homes, one we'd named *Acqua Liana* and the other *Crystalina*. And then—*tap!*—I decided to create two homes that would set the standard for environmentally responsible, luxury construction practices. It was time to innovate and make a market again, to do what nobody else had thought of doing. I was given the chance to rephrase the request from "please help me to get this project financed so I can break into the nine-figure price bracket" to "please help Acqua Liana and Crystalina set the standard for sustainable luxury construction. Help me be the new 'Green Giant.'" I can now see that the first question may have been driven by ego and a strong conviction that I could carry out the initiative, while the second reflected a higher level of social consciousness and will also help me further solidify the Frank McKinney brand.

A close friend shared with me that this same principle of "rephrasing the question" was at work in her personal life when her mother was dying of complications of cancer. She told me how, when she first learned that her mother's illness had advanced to this state, she had felt so helpless, sick to her stomach, and inconsolable. In this state, she wanted to ask God to "fix" it, to take away the cancer, to restore her mother's health. Understandably, she didn't want her mother to die.

When she arrived at her mother's hospital bedside, her distress escalated to the point where she not only felt helpless but useless. *How can I be of any support to my mother like this?* She was dizzy, disoriented, running to the bathroom every ten minutes. She called her pastor from the hospital's chapel. "Help me!" she whimpered into the phone. "I can't be like this right now. My mother and father need me!" Together, my friend and her pastor prayed for strength of body and mind, for clarity of thought, for compassion and wisdom to help her family get through this difficult time. Eventually, she began to feel the nausea lifting, and she was able to return to help make some tough decisions about her mother's care.

She says she thinks this prayer was answered because it was focused on something other than her own pain. She also told me that this prayer, too, evolved from requests for strength to requests for peace for the whole family, to envelop her mother's transition in a sense of safety and the feeling of being deeply loved. In the couple of weeks before her mother died, she began offering prayers of gratitude, too. "Thank you, God, for showing me that I can do this; I can handle this. Thank you for giving me this time to care for my mother in her home, where she's less fearful and we're all better able to prepare for what you have in store. Thank you for this chance to show her my gratitude for the life she gave me. Thank you for the gift of seeing this circle complete with my own flesh and blood. Thank you, God, for your comfort and promise of enduring love."

Of course, she wept when her mother died. She still cries when she talks about it. But this doesn't change the fact that God gave her time and space to *rephrase the question*, and that doing so was one of the miraculous spiritual gifts that came through being present for her mother's passing.

When God Gives You the Finger

All times of perceived silence, no matter how difficult they seem, present you with the opportunity to rephrase the question, to reflect on your motives, to refine your prayers. Notice I didn't say that you should "give up" asking or that you should stop praying. Or that you should interpret the perceived silence as God giving up on you.

It's like that old joke about the flood, where a man decides not to evacuate with the rest of his neighbors and say, instead, that *the Lord will provide* for him. The waters rise, and someone motors up in a boat to rescue him as the man stands at a second-floor window in his house, but the man waves the boat on, insisting that *the Lord will provide* for him. Soon, the man is forced onto the roof, and a helicopter flies over, lowering a rescue worker on a rope to help him. But again the man refuses, saying that *the Lord will provide.*

The man drowns.

As he approaches the Pearly Gates, St. Peter's got his arms crossed and he's shaking his head. "You're early," he says.

"I don't get it!" the man replies. "I thought the Lord would provide for me!"

St. Peter sighs. "Who do you think sent your neighbors, the boat, and the helicopter?!"

We all pray the selfish prayer: "Help *me*, dear God!" And it's perfectly okay to do so. Sometimes God comes to the rescue, giving you the miraculous turnaround in health or wealth or what have you. Yet when it feels as if no help is on its way, it's time to apply the "perceived silence rule" and start looking *inside* for answers and new questions. **It's time to perform what I call a "full soul scan," a complete gut check, and see if you are persisting in a worthwhile direction, or actually resisting God's will for you.** As I described in the previous chapter, sitting down, taking time to be quiet, looking at how you expended your resources and yourself during any given week is incredibly valuable for this. Assessing the cumulative effect over a week or a month or a year can help you notice the signs and patterns (I'm not talking about superstition but rather practical indicators) that show you whether it makes sense to continue on a particular path or not.

Creative persistence is one thing, where you find new ways to meet the challenges thrown at you, refusing to roll over and instead rolling with the punches. Stubborn insistence is another, where you're demanding that God adhere to your timetable and ignoring those practical indicators that may tell you to find a new direction. For me, there are several items on my agenda that I have chalked up to "not yet": the $135 million estate on hold until we get the right financing deal; some wholesome reality-show concepts I've pitched that have been shot down by a few producers who, in my opinion, are short-sighted; a documentary on the green houses we're building that stalled midproduction; my desire to be the thirty-eighth person in the world to finish the Badwater Ultramarathon four or more times; even my dream of becoming the U.S. ambassador to Haiti, which I've not yet actively pursued, nor do I really know how I'd do. I've surrendered all of these to God's timetable, and I have faith that these or, more likely, something better will be given to me when the time's right. *I haven't given up on these plans, though.* I still keep my antennae up in case there's a new opportunity to take a risk and see the eventual reward.

God always answers a sincere prayer. It may not happen in the way that initially asked or as soon as you'd like, but...an answer always comes. The way to ensure that you recognize that answer when it arrives, and don't wind up confused and blaming God like the guy at the Pearly Gates, is to remain sensitive to The Tap. God may very well be giving you the finger, but not in the way that you might think. **God isn't abandoning you, curing you, dismissing you; God is tapping you, calling you, prodding you to find a way to redefine what you want so that it has meaning to someone other than you alone. You *can* have more of anything you desire, as long as you find a way to make that meaningful to someone besides you,** and you stay open to unforeseen ways in which God may deliver exactly what you need, which, as I said, may not look exactly like what you've requested.

The title of this chapter, "Get Off Your Knees and Start Walking" emphasizes that you need to *say your prayers while you're in motion,* looking for opportunities to share what you already have. When the economic environment starts tap-dancing on your business, you can pray walking and consider what resources you can put back into your local community, or even someone else's business. When your love life either dries up or starts to look like a twenty-car pileup, you can pray walking and think about what will put more life and love into the world around you. When the pounds seem to cling to your frame and nothing you do will get you over the plateau, you can pray speed walking and see who could use your help with even the simplest physical tasks. When work seems hard and leisure seems like a fairy tale only other people get to live, you can pray walking and figure out how you can help someone who desperately needs a job.

Pray walking.

Dr. Richard Heinzl, the founder of the Canadian chapter of Doctors Without Borders/*Médecins Sans Frontières,* tells the story of one of his trips to South Africa at the time of the country's first free election in 1994, after the end of apartheid. On the day of the election, he had volunteered to help out at the polling place. He reports that the line was incredibly long, much longer than anyone had anticipated. Over three thousand people came from cities and remote villages to vote for the first time. Because there are many languages in South Africa that have no written representation, the government there had prepared special placards with photographs of the candidates so that those who don't read could still vote. Everyone was allowed to vote, and they were encouraged to do so.

Among those in line at Richard's polling place was a woman in her late eighties, carried by her five sons. She had crippled hands and feet and was unable to walk, so her sons brought her on a blanket, conveying her this way over many miles to reach the voting place. Her family spoke one of the beautiful clicking languages of the area, which has no written form, so they requested a placard for the old woman. When it was brought to her, she reached for it from where she lay on her blanket, and pulled the pictures close so she could be sure of who she chose. Her index finger slowly, painfully extended from her crumpled hand, and she jabbed it decisively at the photo of the candidate she'd chosen.

She affirmed her vote with one word: *Mandela*.

She wept as she handed the card back, and she began repeating a phrase in her native tongue. When someone asked for a translation, her sons said that she was telling them, "I can die now. I have voted."

Because of her persistence and her ability to overcome the fear associated with such a long journey, she had made a way out of no way. Her sons had brought her to this place to cast her ballot in her very first election in the twilight of her life, and this occasion represented not just a chance for her to do something she'd never done before, but also an enormous change for her country. When the former prisoner became president, when Mandela won the election, it was as if he stood on the wreckage of apartheid and showed that the people could rebuild.

Whatever we're given, we're called to make the most of it and to share it with other people. This woman didn't have the ability to walk. She didn't have the ability to read. There were a lot of things this woman didn't have, as she came from a place of extreme poverty. But what she did have was the ability to recognize the man whose face represented freedom to her and to point at that card and say what she wanted.

Ultimately, what this woman represents to me is that you can walk even when it seems you can't. You can take action even when it seems impossible. You can go into new situations, do what's unfamiliar or uncomfortable, and affect someone else's life for the better.

You can build your "tap muscle" while building your tolerance for risk. You can say yes to someone's simple request. You can overcome your fear and your reluctance by starting small. You can pray walking. You can focus on the benefit to someone else instead of yourself and enlarge your sense of mission and purpose in this world. You can be more than your commercial. **You can live a tapped life.**

*　*　*　*　*　*　*

Frank McKinney is a five-time international bestselling author, philanthropist, and extreme risk-taker who's best known for his unprecedented success as a real estate "artist" and visionary. The world's wealthiest clamor for McKinney's masterpieces, with each multimillion-dollar estate inspired by exotic locales and infused with vivid imagination.

McKinney's gift and passion for extraordinary homes extends to his role as the director of the Caring House Project Foundation, a nonprofit he founded in 1998, that provides a self-sustaining existence for some of the most desperately poor and homeless families around the world. CHPF develops entire communities, complete with homes, medical clinics, orphanages, schools churches, clean water, and agricultural assets. McKinney lives with his wife, Nilsa, and their daughter, Laura, in Delray Beach, Florida.

Befriending God
Arathi R. Rao, Ph.D.

It was 5:30AM on a cool Wednesday morning in October. I was driving to the hospital where my husband was about to undergo an emergency quintuple bypass surgery at 7AM. It was pitch dark and I was alone, immersed in my chaotic and fearful thoughts. I was gripped by an icy fear of what could happen to him in the next few hours. Our lives had changed in an instant on that previous Saturday night when, after a pleasant trip to our favorite restaurant, the day had ended with my husband unexpectedly having chest discomfort and being rushed to the hospital. Next morning I was told that his arteries were so severely blocked that he required an emergency quintuple bypass surgery. There was not much time to come to grips with anything. I had all kinds of thoughts racing through my mind such as: Why me? Why us? I felt anger towards God well up inside me. Why was He punishing us? What had we done wrong to deserve this trauma? I was in shock and denial. How could this have happened to my husband at such a young age? His primary care physician only 6 months prior had given him a clean bill of health.

Our 4-year-old twin girls were very scared to see their daddy hooked up to tubes. I was trying to stay calm in front of the kids so as not to worry them, but inside I felt anxious and numb and very fearful. I quickly realized that focusing on 'why' and 'how' this could have happened was futile. I needed to focus on 'what' to do to handle the situation. I focused on getting the best medical care for my husband. I busied myself with making phone calls to physician friends and relatives to get their input. Finally, the decision was made to stay at this hospital for the surgery. I realized later that I was trying desperately to control the situation. I believed at the time that if I attended to every minute detail I would be assured of a favorable outcome. Although I had been praying to God for help, I was not ready to relinquish my need for control or to surrender to Him.

Now the time of my husband's surgery was upon us, and here I was about to walk across the parking lot to go into the hospital. I locked my car and started walking up the short walkway, my entire body tense. Fear and panic began to overtake me as the enormity of what was to come hit me. All my efforts to stay calm and in control were failing. My mind was racing with thoughts of what if I had made a mistake in my choice of surgeon and hospital, what if something went wrong? I felt weak as my veneer of external strength started crumbling. I felt helpless and powerless and realized that there was nothing more I could do to control the situation. It was up to the surgeon and God.

Suddenly, I felt the presence of someone walking beside me. I looked around but there was no one there. Then I sensed the presence of God. He was walking beside me and reassuring me that all was going to be okay with my husband, that He was going to be present in the operating room to guide the surgeon so that the surgery would be successful. If someone had told me a couple of years ago that God would be communicating with me, I would have thought that they had lost their mind. But that day I knew better than to doubt His presence. It was very clear to me that I was not hallucinating, and that God was actually manifesting His presence to me in my time of need. I suddenly felt very calm and comforted as I surrendered to Him my need for control, and the fear that had gripped me earlier melted away completely. I felt my burden lift and I knew instantly that everything would turn out fine. My husband's surgery went well, and he went on to make a total recovery in the following weeks and months. He continues to do well today 10 years later with the grace of God.

As a result of my husband being affected by heart disease, I decided to focus on working with heart patients in my practice. I realized that through this difficult experience, I was being shown my life's purpose, which I had been searching for, for the last several years. Although my work as a psychologist helping people to cope with various emotional challenges had been fulfilling, I had always felt that there was a missing piece. Now, I realized that my life's purpose was to help heart patients and others with medical challenges to empower themselves by harnessing the power of their minds to heal their bodies, minds and spirit.

A cardiac event or any life threatening illness for that matter can have a traumatic and life-changing impact on patients and their families. Over the past several years of working with heart patients, I have found that they, like my husband and I, frequently grapple with a myriad of emotions ranging from shock, denial, anger, depression, loss of control and, most of all, a fear of death. The fear of death and/or fear of having another cardiac event can be crippling and has a huge impact on patients' overall quality of life. This fear can keep a person in the victim's role of feeling helpless and hopeless. In addition, it has been shown that chronic stress and depression can contribute to heart disease and other serious medical conditions. Therefore, it is critically important for a patient to learn effective ways to overcome this fear and anxiety, the most important being to befriend God and surrender to Him in challenging times.

However, in order to be ready to befriend God one needs to overcome one's need for control and independence from God. This is not to say that in times of crisis, we should simply pray and take no action at all. Metaphorically speaking, we need to be in the driver's seat and take appropriate actions, but allow God to be the navigator and guide our actions. We can then gain strength from such a divine collaboration. In order to befriend God it helps to perceive Him as being friendly, loving, accepting, kind, compassionate, and forgiving, instead of stern, intimidating and punitive. One of my former patients, Frank, was helped to cope with his fear of death by befriending God.

Frank had suffered from several heart attacks over a span of just 3-4 years. He was very depressed and anxious. He couldn't sleep at night for fear that he wouldn't wake up in the morning. Frank was very afraid of what would happen to him after death. Frank believed that God was angry with him and that the heart attacks were His way of punishing him for his sins. Frank's fears are typical of many patients who have suffered a sudden cardiac event, or any life threatening illness that brings them face to face with their own mortality.

Frank was helped using guided visualizations, to perceive God as being compassionate and forgiving. He made a remarkable recovery and was able to restfully sleep without fear every night. It's been almost 4 years since I last worked with him, and he continues to do very well having had no subsequent cardiac events. Frank's story is typical of my heart patients who experience a sense of loss of control, grief and fear.

Following are 7 steps you can use to cope with cardiac and other health challenges in your life when you are overcome by fear and anxiety:

1) Acknowledge that there is a Divine Presence/God within and around you.

2) Surrender to this Divine Presence/God your need to control every situation. Get your Ego out of the way and accept guidance. Write out your fears and anxieties on pieces of paper, and put them in a box labeled "Peace Chest" and offer them up to God as a symbolic way of letting go of them.

3) Show Gratitude: Make it a practice to thank God informally several times a day for even small things that go well in your life and make you happy. Take time out to smell the roses and appreciate the gifts of nature.

4) Make a conscious choice to mindfully step out of victim hood and in to self-empowerment with Divine Guidance. Instead of asking "*Why me?*" ask "*Why not me?*" and "*What can I do to cope with this challenge?*" The former question leaves you feeling angry, helpless, hopeless, confused, and victimized. However, the latter question empowers you to reach for your inner strength and faith to cope effectively with your challenges.

5) Seek out the meaning behind your illness by focusing on the changes it has forced you to make in your life. When you discover the meaning and learn from it, you will be in touch with your life's purpose. It can be as simple and yet as profound as learning to take better care of yourself, or becoming a better parent, or helping others who are experiencing similar challenges.

6) Quiet your mind and meditate for 20 minutes each day to relax your body, clear your mind, renew your spirit, and connect with God. Share your thoughts, feelings, and experiences with God without asking for anything in return like you would with a close friend. Just as you cannot hope to be close to someone who you only call upon in times of need, similarly, if you wish to befriend God, you need to develop a similar relationship with Him.

7) Release toxic emotions: Anger and guilt are the biggest destroyers of one's peace of mind. Release guilt by forgiving yourself for past actions and taking appropriate actions to not repeat past mistakes. Release anger by forgiving others. Consciously choose to let go of anger by perceiving it as a toxic substance that destroys you if you hold on to it.

*   *   *   *   *   *   *

Arathi R. Rao, Ph.D., M.A., M.S., M.S.W. is a clinical psychologist practicing in Newtown, Pennsylvania and is on staff at St. Mary Medical Center. Her areas of specialty are wellness, stress management, health and cardiac psychology. Besides maintaining a successful clinical practice, she has provided consultative services to businesses, and conducted stress management workshops in the U.S.A. and overseas. She also does Executive and Life Coaching.

Dr. Rao has been featured in the WHYY-TV 12 "Heart Moments" video on "Stress and Your Heart". She has also been a guest speaker on several radio shows including WWDB, "The Medical View-East Meets West", and WURD Philadelphia talk radio on Stress, Depression and Heart Disease. She is a volunteer spokesperson for the Cardiovascular Institute of Philadelphia.

Who Do You Share Fear With?
Deborah A. Lindholm

My mother and I had a lot of fears in common. In childhood I developed paralyzing fears about dogs, needles and the dentist, which my mother also had. None of these fears had any basis in an actual life experience that resulted in physical harm. In other words, I was never bitten by a dog, extraordinarily hurt by a needle or traumatized by a dentist. Yet, these were debilitating fears that could grip me in the pit of my stomach, start a cold sweat and cause trembling in my body.

At one point as an adult, I began pondering how it was that I had such a fear of dogs. The motivation to question this fear came after visiting a friend's house and feeling foolish about my irrational fear of their dog. Mentally, I posed the question, "Why in the world am I so afraid of dogs?"

Later on, I remembered a childhood event that seemed random at first. In a flash, I recalled the moment my mother and I bonded over our mutual fear of dogs. It happened while we both crouched on top of the hood of a car.

My mother had driven us to her friend's house for a visit. It was in the summer and she parked the car alongside the street nearby. As we emerged from the car, a dog ran off the porch of a house and barked at us. My mother immediately turned around, yanking me back up the street toward the car.

Suddenly, she dropped the idea of getting us back to her car and she jumped atop the hood of someone else's car with me in tow. Her screams for help became louder than the dog's barking. Her friend finally came outside of the house and easily shooed the dog away. We were rescued and drank Kool-Aid on the porch.

I was imprinted with a fear of dogs that day, but never remembered the incident until I began to wonder about where the fear came from. Imprinting is a learning process whereby children develop specific patterns of behavior as a reaction to stimulus from the environment. The patterns of established behavior may or may not have enduring benefit in adulthood and the roots of the imprinting can be long forgotten.

Discovering the roots of a fear is liberating. The additional information paves the way for an individual to make different reactive choices when the fear arises again. When we are aware of being in fear as adults, it is easier for us to engage the conscious mind and evaluate whether the threat at hand is real or not and act accordingly.

As it happens, we normally transition away from the immediate, concrete fears of childhood to fears that are more abstract. These fears may or may not elicit the adrenal fight, flight or freeze responses, but they can certainly wreak havoc with the quality of life and stop you from achieving what you really want. They can be subtle, covered up by excuses and rationalized into denial. Yet, the truth of your fears is always within your grasp if you are not already aware of it.

Long ago, I resolved the childhood fears described here and I also stopped drinking Kool-Aid. Since then I have encountered more serious fears. Much more was at stake like my career, a marriage, financial security, and my health, including a life threatening illness. Consequently, the fears that affected these areas of my life were complex and sometimes it was difficult to understand the root causes.

The circumstances prompted me to develop more skills for handling fears and stimulated the development of a higher consciousness.

As I faced the fears of the past, a simple process began to unfold and I developed a system that brought me great results and feelings of freedom. The expanded premise, principles and steps that follow may be applied to any situation that is holding you back or limiting you through fear.

Freedom from Fear: Declare Your Independence in 5 Simple Steps

Premise: *I hold this truth to be self-evident, that I am endowed by the Creator with the inalienable right to be free from all fear that impedes my independence.*

Principles: *Underlying the process of transcending fears, there are a few key principles that are helpful to keep in mind while handling fears.*

Principle of Divinity ~

It is your divine birthright to live your life free from fear. You were born into a world that offers dualities: polar opposites such as rich and poor, healthy and sick, good and evil, right and wrong, light and the absence of light, love and fear. With the gift of free will choice, you can choose the path of non-duality, which is expansive and relational, supporting a neutral perspective of fear and engaging the higher aspect of self for assistance.

Principle of Manifestation ~

You can manifest from fear or from serenity. As you hold on to fear, that which you fear is fueled to become a self-fulfilling prophecy. Why? Words, thoughts, and emotions have energy. This energy is drawn to like energy. Picture metal shavings on a magnet. The magnet is composed of your beliefs, attitudes and experiences and the metal shavings are the thoughts, emotions and words you currently use that are attracted to the magnet. You draw to you what you think, feel, and say. It is as easy to create a hardship from fear, as it is to manifest a desired goal from serenity.

Principle of Benefaction ~

Fear that is not providing a direct benefit to you limits you and keeps you stuck. It stifles you. It holds you back under false pretenses, rationalizing its very existence with more fears and disastrous "what if" scenarios. Obviously, fear plays a protective and necessary role when we are growing up, filling the data bank in our brain with memories of situations and circumstances to avoid and be wary around for our safety. As an adult, you may rely on fear as a signal to let you know when a situation is dangerous or threatening. Otherwise, consider fear to no longer be your friend and be curious about its hidden agenda.

Principle of Autonomy ~

No one else's fear belongs to you unless you claim it for yourself. We all take on fears through the associations we make via experiences, circumstances and events in life including from our family, workplace, community, culture, other people, the media, and the collective consciousness. Exercise caution when choosing to hold on to a fear. Conversely, no one can make you overcome fear no matter how much they want it for you. You may ask another for assistance, but only your decisions and choices matter. You have total sovereignty when it comes to your fears. You govern yourself.

Principle of Empowerment ~

Transcending fear is empowering. It is liberating and freeing. It builds self-confidence and mastery, helping you to embrace the freedom to pursue your goals and create the life of your dreams. Transcending a single fear has the potential to open up a world of infinite possibilities. It lights the way to territory that you were previously unable to explore. Every fear that you release gives you a new lease on life and attracts opportunities that were previously blocked from your awareness.

Steps and Process

Take the time to write out your answers to the questions below, pondering the challenges in your life and the underlying related fears. As you sit with the questions, your brain will automatically commence sorting to elucidate the answers, allowing you to discover the fears that have limited your progress.

Although the steps are set up in a linear progression, the process itself is nonlinear and the steps can overlap. The process is holistic in nature and you will find that the answers are connected to each other and a theme of fear that is playing out in your life. Likewise, the solutions are inherently part of the process as you notice the patterns occurring.

1. **Evaluate** all aspects of your life - physical, emotional, mental and spiritual.

> What is causing you concern?
> What are you suffering from?
> What is not working in your life?
> What is out of balance in your life?

2. **Proclaim** by stating clearly in positive terms what it is that you want.

> What is most important to you?
> What changes do you want to manifest?
> What do you want to be or have happen?
> What have you yearned for that remains beyond your reach?

3. **Discover** what fears have been holding you back.

> What fear do you want to be free of?
> What are you afraid of losing?
> What could change that causes you fear?
> What reason do you have for keeping the status quo?

4. **Surrender** your fears by mentally releasing them to a higher power—that which you believe in existing above and beyond your ego.

> What is the nature of your relationship with a higher power, meaning God, the Creator, All That Is or the Universe?
> What is hindering your connection with a higher power?

What is the nature of your relationship with the higher aspect of yourself, meaning your soul, Inner Power Source, or High Self?

What is hindering your connection with the higher aspect of yourself?

5. *Act* as if you are free from the fears that have impeded you.

What does it feel like to be free from your fear?

What images and pictures come to mind when you think about being free from your fear?

What do you say to yourself or hear other people say to you when you are free from your fear?

What 3 things can you do in the next 30 days that support the changes you desire?

Dealing with fears is a fact of life. Discovering the fears that are now operating in your life and transcending them one by one is a worthwhile exercise. Each time you handle a false fear and release the underlying illusion, it is enormously freeing. You automatically begin to gain the strength, clarity and wisdom to successfully deal with any fear.

*   *   *   *   *   *   *

Deborah A. Lindholm spent many years in business as a CPA, banker, entrepreneur, and later as a psychotherapist. She holds a Master's in Counseling Psychology-Holistic Specialization. Her interest in holistic principles grew from a serious health issue. In recovering, she awakened to an inner power that transformed her life and connection with the Creator. She co-owns Serenity Matters with her husband Michael. The company is dedicated to empowering clients and students worldwide to awaken their inner power by blending effective coaching techniques with higher consciousness discoveries. To awaken your inner power and surge forward in life, contact Deborah or Michael Lindholm at www.serenitymatters.com.

Remember Your Dream
Gretchel A. Johnson

I didn't realize it at the time, but fear was about to rob me of my dream. It was 1998; I had owned and managed my own day spa business for three years. My dream was to expand since those years had been filled with fun times, a steady flow of clients, and a recurring increase in revenue. I had a passion for helping people feel good about themselves, and discovering their uniqueness (I still do). Of course I would not have been able to do all of that work alone; we were a small team, four service providers in an office building suite a little more than 800 square feet. It didn't take long before we were obviously cramped, toe-to-toe, back-to-back and butt-to-butt. It was time to relocate.

Finding commercial real estate for our needs at that time proved to be a breeze. Within a couple of weeks we had a spot.

Next, I needed to procure a loan…a bank loan that is. None of my friends or family had nonessential funds just hanging around, so I called up my accountant to assist in the process. He had done this sort of thing many times before for his clients. Johnny (not his real name) would make certain all the t's were crossed and all the i's were dotted. We completed the forms and sent them off. Then the waiting began. It was like waiting for a pot of water on the stove to start to boil. It took forever, or so it seemed.

Actually it took about two weeks for the letter to arrive in my mailbox.

With bated breath I opened the letter. It read, "Dear Mrs. Johnson, thank you for choosing…" I knew by the tone at the beginning that my plight would be…DENIED. "Dear God," I remember thinking, "What am I to do now?" All manner of thinking crowded my mind; however, what I wanted most was to arrive at some resolve about the matter… something that would evolve in an affirmative decision to expand, explore and experience serving clients in a new and different way – in a new and different space. This was my DREAM! Now what was I to do? The anguish created doubt about my purpose, and crushed my self-confidence. With my emotions bumping into each other, running all over the place like bumper cars at an amusement park, it would have been easy for me to say, "Forget about it." But what would the staff think? What would the clients say? Would they think I was inadequate to grow the business? The bank certainly didn't have much confidence in my business acumen; I had the letter to prove it. I was frozen in fear.

My mind flashed back to a time when my insightful grandmother courageously faced a would-be intruder, stopping him square in his tracks at our front door and keeping us safe and free from harm. Could I be just as brave? I took notice of my personal environment – I was scared, and I didn't know what to do, but I also knew the power of prayer my grandmother used, as well as some teachings from other sources. I went to work.

First, when I got home that day I meditatively sat down. Secondly, I remembered my goal was to expand my dream. Thirdly, when I was at work I felt the glow of the morning sun flowing in, through, and as me. Next, I felt good just thinking about it - followed by remembering the truth. Finally, I prayed using few words, realizing it wasn't necessary for me to try to use long, flowery words to reach the heart and mind of God. As I finished praying, ending with the last words, in an instant (it doesn't always happen that quickly), I felt no more anguish, fear or despair over the situation. Instead there was a peace - immediately a lightness in the atmosphere enveloped me, so there was no doubt of what I would do next, no doubt at all. That night I got some much-needed sleep – I sensed the next day would be a huge contrast to the day before. I didn't know how it would be different – I just had a "knowing" that it would be. I was grateful for what I imagined would happen.

"You are a co-creator, designed to receive great ideas and make them manifest in the world. They are coming to you specifically for a reason. That reason is: YOU are the person who is supposed to make something good out of them." - Chris Michael **Your Soul's Assignment**

Morning came. I called the vice-president of the bank and respectfully requested an in-person meeting at my location. Incidentally, I didn't reach her right away, but she kindly returned my call before close of business that same day and agreed to the meeting.

In the end, Mrs. Jones (not her real name) came to meet with me. I recall something unusual during our conversation--there was a kind of energy shift when she agreed to take my application (now it had her personal notes written all over it), and then she said her boss would receive it on top of the stack she would present the very next day.

"You don't have to see the whole staircase, just take the first step." – Dr. Martin L. King, Jr.

Finally, after about two weeks had passed, I received a phone call (it was Friday). On the other end Mrs. Jones said, "Mrs. Johnson, I just wanted to make sure you got this message…" I was already about to do the happy dance when she continued, "…Your loan has been approved." I thanked her profusely. After hanging up the phone, with a smile as wide as the entire state of Texas, with unbridled joy and happiness, I yelled, "YES, YES, YES!"

Wait a minute--, let's take a closer look. Isn't fearlessness a state of being in which each of us can tap into? Aren't we uniquely made? Is it possible that desires, goals and dreams are a part of a universal plan? The answer is a resounding YES! Our only job is to remember. Many of us have overcome, walked through, sometimes marched side by side with fear determined to fully experience life, to offer our unique gift/s to the world, to help humanity in some way. It's easy to get thrown off course when fear is strongest, and we're not buckled in for the rough ride, and we're just barely holding on. Come dive into the calm waters of remembering yourself – I have a notion your purpose will appear just beneath the surface. Focus on the "Seven Essentials" for bringing you back to center where you'll feel balanced enough to banish fear, take action, and make your life dance to the music of YES!

Since we all know that fear – like stress - is a part of life, it's also helpful to know that it can be managed, utilizing the right approach, so that we avoid any paralyzing effects, causing dreams to die, relationships to suffer, and careers to fail. The two fundamental effects in the universe, love and fear, are categorized by the emotion you experience at any given time. Like the ones that make you feel good, i.e., kindness, compassion, connectedness, optimism, joy, freedom, peacefulness, and fulfillment – contrast those with the emotions of fear commonly known to make us feel bad such as anger, judgment, jealousy, separateness, abandonment, negativity, pessimism, and vulnerability.

We are familiar with the acronym F.E.A.R., False Evidence Appearing

Real, right? The way it popped up for me symbolized Funneled Energy Aimed in Reverse. The fact is fear's job is to keep us stuck, maintaining the status quo, standing still or looking backwards. We're not talking about the type of fear one experiences in the face of danger, when the body goes into the fight or flight response. Only if there were a lion or similar danger lurking about would this type of fear be useful. No, what we're talking about here is false fear, when there's no danger of you or your loved ones being harmed. It's the kind of fear where we find ourselves in a quandary leasing life, choosing not to enjoy its fullness, rather than living it full out. Having tools and strategies is key for this. Dr. Earnest Holmes writes in ***A New Design for Living***, *"The purpose of our lives is to live life. Do not shy away from it, be fearful of it, or deprive yourself of its full enjoyment."*

There are six steps and one final truth in which to garner a high level of control over fear. I call them **The Seven Essentials**.

1. Identify your desires, goals and/or dreams

- Ask yourself, "What do I want?"

- Write it down.

- Say YES! to feeling good.

2. Uncover values

- What makes you light up?

- Where do you loose track of time?

 - When are you angry?

3. Express Gratitude

- What's working well in your world?

- Focus on your well-being.

- Include helping someone.

- Count at least 3 things for which you are grateful.

4. Sit in Silence

- Sit still.

- Breathe.

- Be quiet.

5. Notice your internal environment

- Identify love or fear.

- What are you sensing in your body?

- Learn to self manage.

6. Create Purposeful Action.

- Put what you have learned into motion.

- Choose how you will handle fear.

- Be accountable.

One truth: YES is the answer. You were born to co-create. It is your nature to love, be happy and healthy. You are always at choice.

Dr. Michael Beckwith speaks of happiness (an expression of love) in *Spiritual Liberation* this way: "Genuine happiness begins when we become conscious that we are co-creators of our destiny with life's source, whether we call it God, the Universal One, or no name at all. Authentic happiness does not come from outer sources; it comes from an inner realization of the Self."

Many others as well as I have used these steps knowing the truth about how to conquer or diminish fear. My soul's desire is to help, assist and support you in remembering your purpose, thus acknowledging YOUR dream.

*   *   *   *   *   *   *

Gretchel A. Johnson, CPCC, ACC, Ph.D., is a twice-certified coach-- both CPCC and ACC are internationally recognized credentials, and the most rigorous in the coaching industry. She is also a doctor of philosophy specializing in holistic life counseling. Gretchel earned a naturopath degree, studied psychology, was a licensed cosmetology instructor, (also owned and managed two salons and one spa for 22 years), and traveled nationally as an educator with a national hair care manufacturer. Gretchel draws from real life experiences, business background, and intuition to help, serve, support and get more deeply in touch with her clients. Working with Gretchel, people learn how to "get unstuck and get moving" as well as identify "hot buttons to kick knee-jerk reactions." You may contact Gretchel in her Bedford, Texas office at 972-741-8723.

When You Want
to Attract Success
Joan Marie Whelan

In order for you to create and attract success into your life, you must be aligned with the "flow" of the Universe. How does one do that and what is the Universal flow? Believe it or not, flowing with the Universe is all about creating your success—they go hand in hand. Flowing with the Universe is being in alignment and feeling comfortable to receive that which you are seeking because you know you deserve it.

So many of us have been set up for the hard road. Our minds automatically go to: *"I can not have that or that is not for me without hard work."* Often times many of us feel that "success and a great life belongs to everyone else but not me". Have you ever felt that way?

Points to examine:
1. What is your belief system focused on? If you seriously desire to succeed at whatever it is you wish to experience in life then it is vital that you re-examine your beliefs and become self-observant. What viewpoint is locked into your belief system and preventing your flow? Is it fear, doubt or unworthiness? Look deep within your soul and see what roadblocks or debris have gotten in the way of your flow. The truth comes down to your personal perception of self and

how much you value you.

2. Where do you place your priorities? If your priority is continually placed on the care and nurturing of others and you rank yourself last on your list, what message are you sending out to the Universe? I believe it would say: *"I am not that important—don't worry about me, take care of everyone else first."* In truth, if you do not feel whole and complete, you are not in the position to help others experience those feelings.

3. Do you feel worthy? If you want to make a lot of money but feel guilty about enjoying the blessings of abundance that money brings, then what are the signals you are giving to the Universe? In life we can only bring into our energy field and manifest that which we not only feel comfortable with having but also that which we truthfully feel belongs to us. Therefore, I encourage you to look into the mirror of your soul and honor what you see. You get to decide what you choose to attract. In the end it always comes down to you—your beliefs and your absolute knowing that you deserve and accept it now.

The only way to success whether it be financial success, healthy living or enjoying loving relationships is through you creating a deep sense of peace within yourself. This must be encircled with links of self-love. You must allow yourself to wake up every day claiming to be the leader you were born to be in this lifetime and believe that you are *"Special"* and have something unique to contribute.

"By becoming a leader of your life, you are empowering yourself to step up and be in charge of your own circumstances." By believing in this statement, feeling the power of this statement and acting upon this statement you are setting yourself up for success. The greatest place to be is in awareness -- even if it means that you have no idea how you

are going to take action. It all starts with you knowing your life has to be different. The moment you make a decision to choose acceptance of your success, the Universe starts placing some things-people or situations on your pathway for you to pick and choose from and waits for you to accept and take appropriate action. Opportunities are placed in front of you and you get to decide if you are going to throw them away because of your fear, doubts and anger or if you are going to trust that there are great possibilities waiting for you to acknowledge and accept. Remember the Universe can only match and bring to you what you on the inside are vibrating to--feeling into and knowing that it belongs to you.

You must become very clear with the meaning of " Who you are and what you want to experience." It is the meaning behind the words that causes us to dig deeper within our soul and look beyond the surface of each situation so we can remain open minded. That's the brilliancy of a successful life. The investment in time and energy that we place on our inner growth is well worth the rewards that you will reap. You must have a sense of your value and self-worth so you can have the strength and courage in any situation to turn your life around. This could mean leaving an abusive situation or moving from poverty to financial stability. It could be going from being single to a relationship. For me, it's about the individual soul's core purpose.

As each day goes by, you'll continue to fine-tune your sense of value and self-worth. Always be open to your own evolution. Don't put yourself in a box. Get creative. Use your imagination and remain open minded as your heart begins to open to the vibration of joyful excitement and recognition of limitless possibilities.

Some key questions to reflect upon as you continue to set yourself up for success are:

1. How passionate are you?
2. How much do you believe in your project and yourself?
3. What is your vision for what you want?
4. What is success to you?
5. What job are you seeking?
6. Are you actively pursuing your opportunities?
7. What is your block?
8. Is there a fear of not being good enough?
9. Is it the fear that you won't succeed and can't step up to the task?

Whatever answers come forward in your mind, I want you to sit with those answers or possible resolutions for a few minutes. Reflect on what your next step is so you will be better prepared to clear the way for a better and happier lifestyle. Visualize this— you are building a fire inside of you in a good way. You are working on revving up your energy as you make positive statements to support your newfound viewpoint. You need to say, *"I won't tolerate negative thoughts or actions anymore."* Breathe out the fear, the doubt and/or feelings of unworthiness. Let them go once and for all and fill your heart with the resources of your source. That is the cleansing work that will help you create your new powerful feelings and positive energy. You need to do some deep breathing and blow out the way these internal and external situations made you feel. Let go and release.

If you have one of my CDs, use that regularly. All of my CDs encompass clearing work.

This exercise really works so I encourage you to incorporate this into your daily life.

Depending upon the depth and degree of your blocks, you may need to sit in meditation daily, drawing on your old memories and confronting them. Step up and say, *"I will not tolerate carrying this energy in my life anymore. I will create a different pattern now because I desire it."*

There is a dance all of us do daily with the Universe. The rhythm and beat of how you feel inside you will dictate your outside circumstances so it is imperative that you learn to dance in unison with that rhythm and beat. Then and only then will you create beautiful music that will resonate with the Universal Flow.

In the last few years, I have grown to realize how my own self worth has dictated my fate. Therefore, I can truly say that I determine my fate. I alone am truly responsible for my actions and my outcome. It took me years to finally realize my true worth and value. I did not think very highly of myself and I accepted the stories and pictures that others tried to attach to me because I did not understand the real meaning. In truth, it was their emotional baggage that they were trying to dump on me. They were actually talking about themselves and I took it as my own. Now I know better and hopefully you do too! This is also what I mean when I say observe—self observe and observe others. We can watch others and observe their emotions, fear and stories but we need not duplicate them as our own.

The Universe has a great deal of patience. It tries to get our attention each and every day. It is up to us to slow down our pace, remove the clutter from our lives and take the time to listen to its soft voice. When we do, miracles happen.

I encourage you to get in touch with your feelings. Our ability to express our feelings is vital to our success. What you feel everyday within you sets the tone of what you will receive in your life. I say to people often you must open your heart more and feel more comfortable receiving. So many want to be in control of everything. Imagine if you could feel vulnerable knowing you are safe and at the same time empowered. Relax, breathe in and focus right now on being relieved because you know you are not alone because the Universal Source truly guides you. What is it you wish to bring into your life? Are you ready to receive it and what does it look like? Are you really prepared? I know we always say yes, I am prepared but too often we are not. Look deep within your soul and see what you need to map out for yourself on a daily consistent basis to allow expansion, growth and success into your life.

When I finally stopped fighting fear and embraced what it had to teach me I surrendered to a new depth of inner peace and contentment and I began creating opportunities in my life that I never thought I could enjoy. I had to let go of what I thought my life was supposed to look like and I decided to open up to the gifts that the Universe wanted to give me.

* * * * * * *

Joan Marie Whelan is the bestselling author of the book *Soul Discovery*. She is an International Lifestyle Makeover Coach, Intuitive who has appeared on numerous radio and TV shows. She continues to travel, speak and teach and has helped several entrepreneurs through her "Lifestyle Programs" to create 7-figure businesses. She consults for many companies and teaches how to create wealth in all areas of people's lives. For more information you can visit Joan Marie's website at: www.joanmariewhelan.com

What's Next?

We'd like to hear from you! What did you think of this book? Did it help? What would you like to learn next? If you let us know, we will gladly continue this discussion as a book series bringing you the best names and the best advice on what matters most. Just go to www. DoneForYouWriting.com/bookseries.htm and send in your questions and comments. In return you'll get access to the recordings of the *How the Fierce Handle Fear* telesummit where we held live trainings on the subject of this book. We hope you'll enjoy it!

About the Editor

Sophronia Scott has over twenty years of experience as a professional writer, most of it spent at *Time* and *People* magazines. When she published her first novel, *All I Need to Get By* with St. Martin's Press in 2004, one prominent reviewer referred to Sophronia as potentially "one of the best writers of her generation." Sophronia holds a bachelor's degree in English from Harvard. As executive editor of The Done For You Writing & Publishing Company, Sophronia helps entrepreneurs and speakers to write and publish books to market their businesses. Her latest work is the award-winning bestseller, ***Doing Business By the Book: How to Craft a Crowd-Pleasing Book and Attract More Clients and Speaking Engagements Than You Ever Thought Possible***. Sophronia can be reached via her website, http://www.doneforyouwriting.com or her blog, http://www.BusinessBytheBookBlog.com.